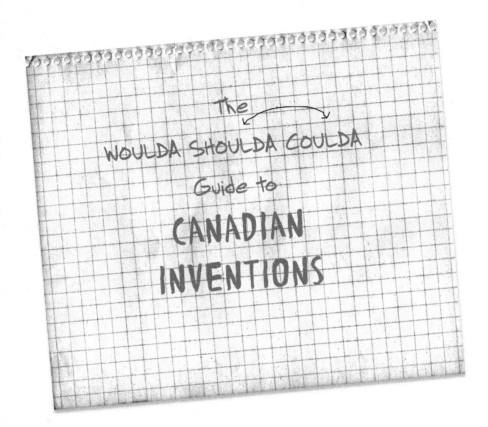

The
WOULDA SHOULDA COULDA
Guide to
CANADIAN
INVENTIONS

Also by Red Green

RED GREEN

The
WOULDA COULDA SHOULDA
Guide to
CANADIAN
INVENTIONS

DOUBLEDAY CANADA

Doubleday Canada and colophon are registered trademarks of Penguin Random House Canada Limited.

Library and Archives Canada Cataloguing in Publication

Smith, Steve, 1945-, author
   The woulda, coulda, shoulda guide to Canadian
inventions / Red Green.

Written by Steve Smith and David T. Smith.
Issued in print and electronic formats.
ISBN 978-0-385-68739-3 (hardcover).--ISBN 978-0-385-68740-9
(EPUB)

   1. Inventions--Canada--Humor. I. Smith, David T.,
1978-, author II. Title. III. Title: Guide to Canadian
inventions. IV. Title: Canadian inventions.

T23.A1S65 2017   609.71   C2017-902474-4
                                            C2017-902475-2

Cover and text design: Leah Springate
Cover art: (photo) Gretchen Gordon; (wood) optimarc; (graph paper) Fotokor77;
(pencil) Gavran333; (flag) Per Bengtsson, all Shutterstock.com
Printed and bound in the USA

Published in Canada by Doubleday Canada,
a division of Penguin Random House Canada Limited

www.penguinrandomhouse.ca

10 9 8 7 6 5 4 3 2 1

Penguin
Random House
DOUBLEDAY CANADA

This book is dedicated to all the past, present and future inventors. You are the Little Engines that Woulda Coulda Shoulda. The ones with the skinned knuckles and the rusty tools and the strained relationships. The people who can think of twenty different ways to get snow off the barn roof but can't get anybody to give them insurance coverage. The folks who have tried to find better, faster, easier ways to do things with no regard for personal gain or safety.

You spend your lives in the optimistic pursuit of the next big thing and often end up losing your savings, your spouse and at least one eyebrow. On behalf of the rest of the world, thanks for your optimism and relentless persistence. Now grab a pair of safety goggles and a fire extinguisher and go invent something.

Quando omni flunkus moritati
(When all else fails, play dead)

—Motto of the Possum Lodge

CONTENTS

The Greatest Not Necessarily Canadian Invention in the World: Candidate #10

The Greatest Not Necessarily Canadian Invention in the World: The Winner

Red Green's Inspirational Quotes for Inventors: Various places throughout the book

FOREWORD

This book is a bit of a puzzle. It's not all fact, but it's not all fiction either. I guess it's what's known as "faction." Many of the inventions featured in here are bona fide, authenticated and factually based innovations. Others come from rumours and stories and urban myths. And rural myths. And myths that have no geographical setting at all.

To avoid confusion and legal action, I've identified the real, actual inventions in a certain way. I'm not going to tell you how, but if you can't figure it out, it's unlikely that you'd be able to mount a convincing case against me. The other stuff, the inventions I'm more or less guessing about, are marked either differently or not at all. Another thing for you to figure out.

I did this on purpose. (My wife says I do *everything* on purpose.) I did it partly for fun and partly because I think it's good to exercise your imagination, but mainly I thought it would give you, the reader, a sense of what it means to be an inventor.

To get the most out of this book and get to the end successfully, you'll need to stay focused and pay attention to the information you're getting and, most important, be able to sort the solution from the pollution. Have fun and learn something—and, above all, keep your stick on the ice.

Red Green

INTRODUCTION

I don't think the rest of the world completely understands
Canadians. We have a reputation for being nice. We're tolerant,
apparently. We don't whine about everything, we give people the
benefit of the doubt, we don't spend our days looking for an
argument, we go along to get along.

I think that's all more or less true, but it's not the whole picture.

When a person doesn't complain, it doesn't mean they think
everything is perfect. When we're not looking for an argument, it
doesn't mean we agree with everything. When we're not looking
for a fight, it doesn't mean we won't fight. When we go along to
get along, that's us extending the hand of friendship.

When you live in a country that's bigger in size than the U.S.
but with only the population of California, you need to get along
with everybody or you'll run out of friends in a hurry.

The world has been reminded on a few occasions that they
shouldn't mistake our kindness for weakness. Take the World
Cup of Hockey, for example.

Along the same lines, just because we don't brag doesn't mean
we're not proud. And that's where this book comes in.

We're proud of our inventors. And for a country with so few
people, our ability to generate so many world-class inventors tells
me we must be doing something right. When we see flaws in the
world around us, instead of whining about it, we figure out a way
to make it better. I like that about us. As you go through this book,
think about how all of these inventions, from the paint roller to the
cardiac pacemaker, have made life better for all of us.

Give yourself another reason to be proud of Canada. Just
don't tell anybody.

ALKALINE BATTERY
Lewis Urry

Lewis Urry was born in Pontypool, Ontario, in 1927 and was the first guy to be able to make an alkaline battery that could last longer than the zinc-carbon battery everybody was using in their three-pound metal flashlights.

Sometime in the 1950s Lewis came up with the nifty trick of using manganese dioxide, solid zinc and powdered zinc alongside the alkaline, which somehow allowed the battery to last much longer. Attaboy, Lewis. In the 1950s, while you were doing experiments that made you a millionaire, I was playing with my Gilbert chemistry set, making the basement smell like rotten eggs and taking thermometers apart so I could watch the mercury roll around in my hand.

When the alkaline battery patent was granted to Lewis and his team in 1960, that was what I would call a good day. The company, Union Carbide Corporation, later was renamed Energizer. Perhaps you've heard of them. Meanwhile, the Gilbert chemistry set folks went under.

✳ ✳ ✳

At first many Lodge members thought these were Al Kaline batteries. As you know, Al Kaline played right field for the Detroit Tigers. Lodge members were shocked to think that Al Kaline had enough time to invent a battery, but they always say right field is the easiest position. The biggest surprise to them was that they thought that meant he was Canadian. Whenever you hear a Lodge member say stuff like that, you're reminded of why Google was created.

Maybe the whole world made a big mistake when they demoted batteries from a primary, and sometimes only, source of energy to become either a portable form of electricity or a backup plan for those times when the power goes off because of either a failure in the ability of the power grid to generate electricity or a failure in the ability of the homeowner to pay the electric bill.

Al Kaline—Mr. Tiger

If instead of wiring the nation and making us all dependent on ever more costly generated electricity, they had continued to make more and more powerful and efficient batteries that could be charged by the sun, we'd be free and happy and masters of our own destiny and nobody would have to live under high-tension wires that make their fillings hum.

(There's a whole episode of my show devoted to the idea of turning Possum Lake into a battery. It's on the Book of Inventions page at redgreen.com. Click on "Battery.")

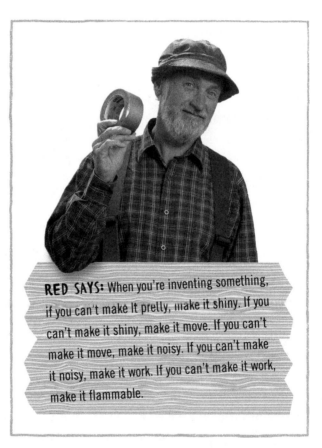

RED SAYS: When you're inventing something, if you can't make it pretty, make it shiny. If you can't make it shiny, make it move. If you can't make it move, make it noisy. If you can't make it noisy, make it work. If you can't make it work, make it flammable.

AM RADIO
Reginald Fessenden

Reginald Fessenden, who also invented sonar (see page 194), is the guy who put out the first-ever AM voice transmission in 1900. My guess is he did it in the morning. Otherwise it would have been a PM voice transmission.

On Christmas Eve, Reggie did a broadcast in which he played "O Holy Night" on the violin and then sang the third verse. And before the applause could die down, he played a recorded song while he read the Jesus-in-the-manger scripture from the gospel according to Luke. If he had given out a phone number, it could have been the first-ever PBS pledge break.

Despite his attempts at creating popular programming, Fessenden was a key player in the development of AM radio from that point until 1920, when it really took off. When Reggie came on board, AM radio was all done with Morse code, but he switched that over to voice, which was much better. "O Holy Night" is not nearly as good in Morse code. I'm sure he had no idea where AM radio would go by the 1950s or he would have called himself Wolfman Reginald.

* * *

 To me, this is one of those inventions that's more than a thing. It's a life changer. At least it was for anyone in my age bracket. How could you possibly go on a picnic or spend a day at the beach or pretend to do your homework without that AM transistor radio pumping out the Top Forty? I even had one that hung from the handlebars of my bike. Of course, that was in the days when people wouldn't steal your radio. Or your bike. Or the bench it was chained to.

And despite Reggie singing hymns and reciting from the Bible, the real purpose of AM radio was to promote rock 'n' roll. You weren't gonna hear no boogie-woogie from the philharmonic or the church choir.

I'm even old enough to remember sitcoms and variety shows on the radio. *Our Miss Brooks*, *Burns and Allen*, even *Ted Mack's Amateur Hour* could hold your attention without the need for lighting or makeup or special effects. That's because the producers thought the listeners were smart enough to create the pictures in their own minds. Eventually, they realized that almost everybody's stupid so they invented television.

I say Reg deserves a lot of credit, and I don't mean this to sound insensitive, but why does AM radio still exist? It sounds crappy, lots of static, mainly people talking and there are a million stations about 1/100th of a dial turn apart.

It seems to me that we have too many kinds of radio anyway—AM, FM, CB, HAM, SAT, etc. Surely it's time to simplify. Let's start with HAM and CB, or as they're called now, the cell phone. They can go. That leaves AM, FM and SAT. Of those, SAT is the only one that covers the whole country at once. You can tune into your favourite satellite station in St. John's and listen to it continuously as you drive to Vancouver.

What you don't get is any local news or opinion or local flavour of any kind.

That's where FM comes in, or at least could come in, if it was being done right. FM supplies a strong, clear signal with a full frequency range. No static. No interference. No tinniness. No muffled tones. Music sounds great on it. Dialogue is clear. Last, but *not not* least, is AM. It has terrible sound and a weak signal.

As my dad used to say when my uncle would come to visit, why is it still here? AM should have been kyboshed about forty years ago, with the invisible hand of Adam Smith flicking it off the menu. So what gives?

Regardless of how crappy the reception is, if you want to hear local news or sports or weather, you've got to go to AM. It's all a management issue, and these guys must be in cahoots. They must have this code that dictates what kind of content goes where. If they have a program with an interesting, informed, energetic host talking about stuff you care about, they put it on AM. If they have a program that features an airhead with a deep voice presenting love ballads, they put it on FM.

So as a listener, you've got two options: you can either listen to the AM show that is interesting but really hard to hear, or the FM show that is mind-numbingly boring but comes in clear as a bell.

Oh sure, I guess in the old days you could say that a lot of people didn't have an FM radio but everybody had an AM radio. Well, that's just not true anymore. They haven't built a car without an FM radio since Lada went under. Even garbage trucks have FM radios.

The real reason we still have AM radio is human nature. Very few things in life disappear forever. You may think things come and go, but the truth is once they're here, they tend to stay, but in a limited capacity. There are still blacksmiths and phone booths and lava lamps and butter churners and television antennas and flavour straws and door-to-door salesmen and Silly Putty. Once we get used to something, we don't like to ever completely forget about it. We just put it off to the side while we use the newer, better thing. But the old thing is still there, in the garage behind the stack of encyclopedias.

Maybe we don't want anything to be forgotten because we could be next. That must be the reason AM radio is still with us. Right now, everything I want to listen to—news, weather, sports, etc.—is on AM radio, but everything that sounds good is on FM. Fortunately for me, my hearing is going, so that's levelling the playing field a bit. And with AM you get variety. With FM, you get a hundred stations playing three different kinds of music.

If anybody had the guts to take four of those hundred FM stations and give each of 'em an AM-type format—local news, live sports, local weather and car talk—they would be number one with a bullet.

ANTI-GRAVITY SUIT
Wilbur R. Franks

Wilbur R. Franks was born in Weston, Ontario, on March 4, 1901. He graduated from the University of Toronto and went over to the Banting Institute, still on campus, to be a cancer researcher. During his experiments he noticed that when he was spinning test tubes, they would often crack from the strong centrifugal force, and Wilbur wasn't the kind of guy to take cracked test tubes lightly. Or anything lightly. He fixed the problem by first sticking the test tubes in larger, liquid-filled bottles. It worked.

This got Wilbur thinking about how being surrounded with water reduced outside forces like gravity. He was aware that when airplane pilots are under high g-forces, they would often black out, which was inconvenient. Wilbur figured that at least partially surrounding them in liquid could prevent bad things from happening, so in 1940 he came out with the Franks Flying Suit, which was made of rubber and water-filled pads. It worked great and was used regularly by pilots in World War II.

Eventually the design got even better and became the anti-gravity suit worn by astronauts and cosmonauts around—and above—the world.

These suits should not be confused with Eddie's Ralphing Suit, worn in case of vomiting at stag parties. It didn't prevent anything, but it was easy to clean.

✳ ✳ ✳

 It requires a special kind of person to take on the natural forces of the universe. Not that Wilbur thought he could completely overpower the forces of gravity, but he sure believed he could knock them down a peg or two. He obviously had a pretty healthy ego.

Mother Nature can be a difficult date. We get a few minor victories like sunblock to prevent burning or spillways to prevent flooding, but so far nobody has come up with a way to move precipitation or reduce wind or unscrew a tornado. Maybe one day—who knows?

Maybe one of you kids out there will come up with a way of reducing the intensity of lightning by channelling it through a dimmer. But before you touch that lightning knob, I suggest you slip on about seven pairs of rubber boots.

Twenty years before Mr. Franks's invention, local flyer Gwen Morrisburg had been working on the same problem. She would often do tricks at county fairs, most of which were in an airplane, and she noticed that when she was pulling out of steep dives, or crawling out of local dives, she would often feel light-headed to the point of almost losing consciousness. However, if it was during a time when she was retaining water, she was fine, although usually everybody else wasn't.

Just like Wilbur, she figured that surrounding the body with fluid would stop the forces of gravity. Unlike Mr. Franks, she didn't think of having pockets of water in her outfit, but women don't like pockets anyway.

Instead she purchased two rubber diving suits. One was exactly fitted to her figure; the other was seven sizes too large. She

Gwen Morrisburg, Possum Lake Fly Girl

put the big one on over the small one, sealed the wrist, ankle and neck holes with plumber's putty and then filled the space between the suits with raspberry gelatin. Overtop she wore a loose-fitting cotton dress (as pictured above) for modesty. She insisted on wearing a matching hat. She thought it made her look slimmer, but maybe not the best choice for a stunt flyer. She went through a lot of hats.

The first time she tried the anti-gravity outfit was at the Possum Lake County Fair of 1923. As soon as she was suited up and got the dress on, she sat in the plane in a cool, dark place, waiting for the jelly to firm up. After it did, she yelled over to the tower that she was "all set." That may have been the first time a person's butt firmed up by just sitting on it.

She took off and started through her routine. She did steep dives and barrel rolls without the slightest twinge of light-headedness. However, when she did the upside-down flypass, her dress flipped up over her head and the entire crowd fainted.

BASKETBALL
Dr. James Naismith

Dr. James Naismith, born in 1861 in Almonte, Ontario, is recognized as the guy who invented the game of basketball. He came up with it in 1891 when he was teaching at a YMCA. Naismith lived to see basketball dribble and bounce and eventually break away into a college, professional and even Olympic sport. Although he never once dunked.

Red and Jimmy shooting hoops in Mono Mills, Ontario

✳ ✳ ✳

Inventing a game is really easy to do. My uncle used to invent games every few days. They were dumb games and had stupid rules that didn't make any sense and he could never get anybody to play them, and he was eventually put on medication and taken to a special place—but the point is that inventing a game is the easy part. Making it a good enough game that catches on and flourishes is the tough part.

People have been inventing games for five thousand years and although the world now has a population of more than seven billion, there are fewer than fifty games that could be called popular. You do the math. I certainly can't. But I know that the game-invention business must have a really high failure rate. So congrats, Jimmy, you beat the odds with a small ball, a medium-sized basket and a big dream.

By pure coincidence, at about the same time Naismith was creating basketball, local sports enthusiast and part-time Possum High phys. ed. teacher Butch Dempster was developing something very similar.

As with so many great inventions, it started with a problem. Each year when the fall school term began, all of the stronger, more athletic boys went into hockey. They practised day and night because for many of them it was their best and only career choice. For Butch, this meant that the only boys left to attend his gym classes were unathletic, wimpy and pretty much useless at sports.

Rather than bullying and ridiculing them, which had never worked for him in the past, he decided to let three of the suckiest boys create their own game and try to come as close to hockey as possible. They sat in a circle in the middle of the gym and discussed how the game would go. Butch threw out the challenge to the boys and then just sat back and wrote down their suggestions.

Bernard "Butch" Dempster,
Undershirt Model

BOY #1: No puck. It can't use a puck. Pucks are hard and small and are the main reason hockey players don't have teeth.

BOY #2: Okay, so how about a ball? A *big* ball.

BOY #1: Not a bowling ball.

BOY #3: An inflatable ball. About the size of a soccer ball, but more rubbery, so if it hits you on the head it will bounce off instead of it fracturing your skull and your brains all seep out through your ear.

BOY #2: And it needs to be orange . . . For luck.

(Uncomfortable pause)

BUTCH: This doesn't sound much like hockey.

BOY #1: We'll make it five boys on each team. That will make it exactly like hockey.

BUTCH: Hockey has six on a team.

BOY #1: Yes, but we're not going to have a goalie. Makes it too hard to score.

BUTCH: I don't think that's the reason why you find it hard to score.

BOY #3: And we'll have a goal, just like hockey—but not a square goal because it has corners and you can hurt yourself badly on a corner. We'll use a clothes hamper, and you throw the ball into it. It'll be like laundry day in the boys' residence.

BOY #2: And we'll have penalties, just like hockey.

BOY #3: Lots of penalties.

BOY #1: Way more penalties than hockey.

BUTCH: What kind of penalties? Boarding? Cross-checking? Fighting?

BOY #1: No. None of that.

BOY #2: Are you crazy? Are you trying to get us killed?

BOY #3: No checking of any kind. Ever.

BOY #1: No touching.

BOY #3: Even better. No touching.

BUTCH: What about eye contact?

BOY #1: We'll let it slide for a while and see how it goes.

BUTCH: Walk me through how the game would work.

BOY #1: Well, the two teams would line up at centre court, like they do in hockey. But no faceoffs. You know it's a violent sport when the first thing you do is try to rip somebody's face off.

BOY #3: We'll have a jump ball. The referee will throw the ball up in the air.

BOY #1: It's inflated.

BOY #2: And orange.

(Uncomfortable pause)

BOY #3: One of the teams catches the ball and runs down the floor and throws it into the laundry hamper.

BUTCH: Any passing?

BOY #2: Only if absolutely necessary.

BOY #1: If anybody touches you, that's a foul.

BUTCH: You mean touches the ball carrier?

BOY #2: No. We mean touches anybody. At any time—before the game, in the schoolyard . . . anywhere. No touching.

BUTCH: And what happens when you toss the ball into the laundry hamper?

BOY #1: Game's over. We'll be exhausted and ready to get back to our homework.

And so the game of wussball was invented. It never really caught on. Even the boys who invented it wouldn't play. But if you watch a professional basketball game today, the similarities are startling.

To watch our Adventure Film on basketball, go to the Book of Inventions page at redgreen.com and click on "Basketball."

THE BLACKBERRY
Mike Lazaridis

Mike Lazaridis was born in Istanbul, Turkey, in 1961. At the age of five he moved with his family to Canada, where they put down roots in Windsor, Ontario. At age twelve, he read every science book at the public library in Windsor, and received a prize for the effort. And yes, it was more than three books. Not sure what the prize was, but I'm hoping it included an agreement not to tell any of Mike's twelve-year-old buddies.

In 1979, he began an electrical engineering degree, with an option for computer science, at the University of Waterloo. In 1984, Lazaridis heard about a request for proposals from General Motors concerning a network computer control display. Mike submitted a proposal and GM awarded him a contract. They were doing better in those days.

With just two months left till graduation, he made the tough decision to drop out of school to start work on the contract. The GM contract, a small government grant and a loan from Mike's parents enabled Lazaridis, Mike Barnstijn, and Douglas Fregin to launch Research In Motion. (They were going to name it Research Standing Still if the government got more involved.) One of the company's first major achievements was the development of barcode technology. Apparently it caught on. RIM used the profits to research wireless data transmission. Result: the BlackBerry mobile device in 1999, and its better-known version in 2002.

✳ ✳ ✳

 I like hearing about inventions and the reason they came into being and all the hurdles the inventor had to get over, but the thing that fascinates me the most is how they come up with a name for the invention. Most of them make sense, like paint roller and snowblower and hearing aid, but they're boring. Then along comes the BlackBerry.

"Okay, let's see . . . we've got a device that works like a phone but can also send and receive files, pictures and messages. What should we call it? The Communicator? The Internetcom? The Superphone?"

"No, no, I think we should go with the BlackBerry."

"Really? Why?"

"I like blackberries."

"Yeah, okay, but a blackberry is like a little fruit that's pretty ugly and a bit on the sour side."

"Yeah but I like 'em."

"Okay, so you wanna give it a fruity name. What about the Nectarine?"

"I like the BlackBerry."

"Yeah, I get that. I just don't get the connection to the product."

"Well, it's small and black and is always low on juice."

Inspired by the BlackBerry, Alex Rifkin, a local guy with big ideas and time on his hands, decided to create a similar communication device that would not require any cellular or Internet connections.

As a child, Alex had learned how to play a small wind instrument that everybody called a "sweet potato." At least that's what they called it to his face. But it's real name was "ocarina".

He was fascinated with its design and in later years raised enough money to build a community centre shaped like a giant sweet potato. He called it "The Giant Sweet Potato Community Centre" but the town council demanded a more subtle reference to the design of the building so they changed the name later that afternoon to "The Oak Arena". At this point Alex felt a need to express his masculinity by abandoning the sweet potato and moving up to the more manly piccolo.

Alex Rifkin, Local Developer and Freelance Piccolo Player

After years of practice he became one of the better piccolo players in the Possum Lake area. He auditioned for a couple of heavy metal bands but it was never really a fit. He also tried to use his musical ability to meet women. On two separate occasions he tried the pick-up line "Would you like to see my piccolo?" Neither went well.

While practising one day, Alex noticed that if he played a very high note at full volume, he would get complaints from neighbours way beyond his own trailer park. That was when he got the idea to use the instrument for communication.

Alex knew that every musical note is identified with a letter. When a musician reading music sees the letter, he converts it to a note. It only makes sense that when a musician hears the note, he'll be able to convert it back to a letter. That became the founding principle of the WhistleBerry—a device that communicates using high-pitched, high-volume musical notes.

Alex added a small-format cassette recorder that hung down below the piccolo and allowed the user to record messages and play them back later. Despite the brilliance of the plan, there were a couple of drawbacks. First problem was the limited range— many musicians are smokers and don't have the lung power to send a WhistleBerry message across town. Even with a full set of powerful lungs, long-distance calls were out of the question.

Alex toyed with the idea of adding mechanical amplification, but he found that strapping a gas-powered air compressor to the customer's back really cut into the portability of the unit. And even for short distances, wind was an issue. At one point Alex was accidentally locked in his bathroom during a tornado and the WhistleBerry wasn't even loud enough for his wife to hear. Although she said she never listens to anything he does in there.

But the biggest issue was the limited vocabulary. There are only seven notes in a musical scale, so that meant the messages were limited to seven different letters—A, B, C, D, E, F and G. Even an experienced Scrabble player had trouble creating usable communiqués. Initially, Alex tried to communicate with just one note at a time—for instance, a B-sharp was code for "smarten up," and an F-flat meant that girl wasn't worth pursuing.

But besides being offensive, this approach was very limiting, so Alex fixed the problem by creating a more elaborate code that would allow for better and more secure messages:

DEAD BEEF meant "We're having pot roast tonight."
CABBAGE FACE meant "Your boss is looking for you."
ADDED BED meant "I have filed for a trial separation."

Sadly, if the recipient didn't have perfect pitch, he would misunderstand the message. Alex sent a message to one of his assistants, who turned out to be tone deaf and showed up at Alex's house an hour later with a forty-five-gallon drum of personal lubricant. Despite his best efforts, Alex's WhistleBerry was doomed from the beginning, or maybe even slightly before. The entire adventure was reduced to one more whistle-stop on his road to ignominy.

RED SAYS: As an inventor, you're limited only by your own imagination and the bylaws in your area.

GREATEST INVENTION IN THE WORLD

CANDIDATE # 1 | The Calendar

C alendars have been around for a long time. Ever since the first caveman forgot his wedding anniversary, this tool has been keeping human beings organized and efficient and on time.

The first calendars came out in the Bronze Age, which was a while ago. Then Julius Caesar did a 2.0 version in about 45 BCE. These early calendars were based on what was happening in the sky, which in those days wasn't much. The movements of the sun and the moon and maybe a planet or two was about it. No space shuttles or 747s or drones. But as soon as scientists started figuring out how the earth moves inside the solar system, the calendars got a lot better and more popular. Such developments as bikinis, firemen and airbrush photography haven't hurt either.

But no matter how good calendars get, they're still no help to those of us who forget to put the upcoming event onto the calendar in the first place. This is really the Achilles heel of the calendar system: you still have to do something. Men hate that.

RATING: Nice try, but not the greatest invention in the world of all time ever. Watch for Candidate #2, coming up later in this book.

BLOODY CAESAR
Walter Chell

This alcoholic drink was invented by a guy in Calgary named Walter Chell. At the time, he was the restaurant manager of the Calgary Inn, which later became the Westin Hotel. In 1969 the hotel was opening a new Italian restaurant, and Walter was told to come up with a signature drink for it. He eventually decided to put vodka, Clamato juice, Worcestershire sauce, celery salt, celery, Tabasco sauce, ice cubes and a lime wedge together in a tall glass, and the Bloody Caesar was born. It caught on right away and has become Canada's national cocktail. I'm guessing Molson Canadian is the national chaser.

✳ ✳ ✳

As this book demonstrates on almost half of the pages, there are some amazingly creative people in this world. And none more so than in the field of naming alcoholic mixed drinks. Moscow Mule, Golden Cadillac, Dark and Stormy Night, Tequila Sunrise,

Screwdriver, Sex on the Beach. Really makes you wonder what they were doing when they named the drink. And how was the drink involved with the activity? Was it consumed during or maybe after, as a celebration? Or maybe the drinks came first and were the *cause* of the activity. But when you look at all these drink names, the "Bloody Caesar" has to be a standout. My guess is that this cocktail is the only one named after a political assassination. There's no "Night Out with Lincoln" or the "Grassy Knoll" or the "Jell-O Shot Heard Round the World."

Isn't calling a drink a Bloody Caesar a little insensitive? And coming from Canada too. Canada is the last place you'd expect to find a violent, revolutionary drink name. We're peaceful here. We've never had a prime minister spoken rudely to, much less assassinated. We didn't even really rebel against Great Britain, we just moved out.

Generally speaking, Canadians aren't vicious killers or mercenary opportunists, so I think this is one of those cases where people just look at it as a catchy name without considering what it really means.

So I've done the thinking for you. It's called "bloody" because of the colour of the Clamato juice and also to make you think of a Bloody Mary, which was already a popular drink—always smart to latch on to somebody else's fame. Like Elvis impersonators do. And I guess the "Caesar" part is because it was an Italian restaurant with a Canadian spin. Sort of an Eh-tu, Brute.

So the name Bloody Caesar is just a fun, catchy name that Canadians like, and when they drink it they're not thinking about being stabbed to death by their best friends and left to die on the steps of the bar.

CANADA DRY GINGER ALE
John J. McLaughlin

John J. McLaughlin was born on March 3, 1865, in Enniskillen, Ontario. His father was Robert McLaughlin, who started the car company that eventually turned into General Motors of Canada. My dad used to talk about a McLaughlin Buick. It was either the same McLaughlin or an unbelievable coincidence. So I guess John was thinking, "Anybody can make a car, but very few can come up with a half-decent soft drink."

John graduated from the Ontario College of Pharmacy in 1885. He travelled around Europe, where he got his first taste of the old-style golden ginger beer they drank over there. He must have gotten pretty excited about it, because when McLaughlin returned to Toronto in 1890, he gave up the pharmacy business and opened a soda-bottling plant, making his version of what he'd been drinking in the motherland. I guess the Europeans couldn't stop him or didn't bother trying. Maybe they weren't aware that Canada was a country.

In 1904, McLaughlin's company came out with the first-ever "dry" ginger ale, under the name Canada Dry. It caught on right away. They were selling way more "dry" than "golden." Pretty soon it was for sale across the country and beyond. When they were looking for a slogan, I would have suggested "Ginger ale is like your pants—better dry." But instead they went with "The Champagne of Ginger Ales," and it continues to this day to be the most popular ginger ale in North America.

Yet another brilliant Canadian who understood the value of not starting from scratch. Way smarter to find a good product and improve it than to try to come up with a new idea. A good idea is always better than a new idea, except when they're both, which doesn't happen all that often.

So J.J. found a popular drink, ginger beer, and decided that if he could jimmy the formula enough to get a patent, without abandoning the basic brand, he'd have a winner. I'm sure the fact that he was a chemist didn't hurt.

As far as I can tell, he did two things right. First, he figured that ginger beer could afford to be a lot less sweet, and second that the word *dry* is the key, because it is a nice word for "sour" and it's used when you're talking about wine. So instead of calling his new drink Canada Sour, he called it Canada Dry, which was smart, but adding the tagline "The Champagne of Ginger Ales" was inspired.

Suddenly, anybody with $1.29 could buy a bottle of champagne at their local 7-Eleven. Let's pop the bubbly and give Mr. McLaughlin a toast. A dry toast.

✳ ✳ ✳

 It's somewhat interesting that people have always had a thing for beverages. Wine in the Bible, mead in the Middle Ages, sarsaparilla in the Old West, and Vernor's Ginger Ale for about two weeks in the early '60s. For hundreds of years, doctors have told us we need to drink more water, but we don't want to. That's because many of us lived in Brantford. Water is too bland.

I think most people prefer eating to drinking, so when they drink, they want it to feel like eating. There needs to be some substance and flavour and physical sensation. Drinking water is not like eating, it's like breathing liquid air. There's no kick, there's no feeling, there's no fun.

Booze has all of those in spades. But you don't want to be drinking alcohol all the time. Especially if you're a motorcycle cop. Coffee has the kick, but no feeling and no fun. Fruit juice has the feeling and the fun, but no kick. Then along came the miracle of carbonation. The soft drink. Kick, feeling *and* fun. So many of us have great teenage memories of sitting in the soda shop, chugging a large Coke and letting out a belch that shook the light fixtures and made everybody's eyes water. That's living, baby.

Local Lodge member Floyd Demsler admired McLaughlin and spent most of his life—and all of his wife's money—trying to emulate his success. Floyd was fascinated with bubbles, to the point that it eventually became his nickname. Even as a boy he would often slip away to the bathroom with a box of baking soda and a quart of vinegar. He would count and measure the bubbles and try to find a connection between the chemicals involved.

Floyd "Bubbles" Demsler, Carbonation Specialist

He became an expert on the bubbles in Canada Dry and some other carbonated beverages, although he never figured out where the bubbles in the bathtub were coming from. But he had his suspicions. When Floyd saw the success of Canada Dry, he was determined to make a similar beverage. Since ginger was a root plant, Floyd started with carrots and gradually worked his way through the family of underground spices and legumes. His Parsnip Soda and Pumpkin Pop were immediate failures, but when he came out with his Turnip Dry Ale, the public turned to violence. A gang of hoodlums broke the windows of his lab with bottles of his own Cauliflower Cola and the even less popular Diet Cauliflower Cola. They smashed all of Floyd's equipment and then beat him about the upper arms with a medium-sized eggplant. Floyd survived the attack but abandoned his dream of cornering the vegetable-based soft drink industry.

Instead he turned his hand to making alcoholic drinks. His Brussels Sprout Lager and Yam Pale Ale never really caught on, but people say his Green Pea Beer sure lived up to its name.

To see how we made our beer at the Lodge, go to the Book of Inventions page at redgreen.com and click on "Beer."

RED SAYS: Invent a better mousetrap, or miss a few car payments, and the world will beat a path to your door.

CANADARM
DSMA Atcon

I n 1969, NASA found out about a robot being made by a Canadian
company called DSMA Atcon. They were using the robot to load fuel into
CANDU nuclear reactors. It was hard to find workers willing to pick up
handfuls of plutonium and toss 'em into a hopper. Especially workers who
were hoping to have a family. Or only one head.

NASA was impressed and invited Canada to get involved with its
space shuttle program. To be exact, NASA was looking for some help with
the Shuttle Remote Manipulator System. It took a few years of work, but
eventually Spar Aerospace, along with subcontractors Dynacon of Toronto
and CAE Electronics of Montreal, made the Canadarm and delivered it to
NASA in 1981.

If they had built two, they could have used each of them to load the other onto the train. And then perform the greatest high five ever recorded. But no.

✳ ✳ ✳

 People—mostly men—have always liked the idea of getting someone else to do the work. If you can't find a friend or can't afford a valet or can't afford a friend, the next best thing is a robot. If you can't afford a robot, the next best thing is part of a robot. In this case, an arm. Even the cavemen knew the value of a robot arm. In their case, it was a club, but isn't it a lot smarter to prod a sabretooth tiger with a club than with your formerly five-fingered hand?

Sure, the Canadarm is pretty fancy, but it owes a lot of its basics to the shepherd's crook and the mariner's boat hook. Take a long, hard look at the picture on page 33 and tell me that doesn't look like a high-end golf ball retriever. Although if your golf ball ends up in space, it may be time to take up a different game.

And as usual, tools and software that were meant for the space program can make our lives better right here on earth, or whatever planet you live on. Wouldn't it be great to have your very own Canadarm right there for you to use in your own home? We'd have to make a few modifications in terms of size and weight, but the basic engineering remains the same.

And think of the convenience of having a Canadarm at your fingertips. Batteries dead in your remote? No problem. Use the Canadarm to push the buttons on the TV. Have a disgusting load of dirty laundry? No problem. Toss it all into the washing machine using your Canadarm. Want to grab another hot potato from the far end of the table?

Well, you get the idea. I know you're excited, so let's get started.

The Canadarm has three separate motions: extension, rotation and compression. The arm extends until it's close to an object, rotates to put the pincers in the right position and then

compresses the pincers to pick up the object. So let's deal with those motions one at a time. We'll start with extension. Are there any tools out there that could be repurposed into a device that's capable of changing its length? Of course there are, and you've probably already guessed what I'm thinking: a cordless drill and a house jack.

A house jack is a tube of steel with a nut welded onto one end. A threaded rod connected to a flange runs through that nut. It works by using the mechanical advantage of the low pitch of the threads. By turning the threaded rod, the flange is forced to rise and lift the house resting on it. It may sound impossible, but remember that you're not really raising the house—the house has sunk for some reason. All you're doing is putting it back the way it's supposed to be.

But let's get back to our Canadarm. First step is to remove the flange from the end of the rod. It may pop off easily, but if not, smack it with a sledgehammer or drive over it repeatedly.

Once the flange is gone, tighten the chuck of the cordless drill over the end of the threaded rod.

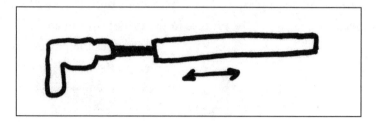

You have now changed the house jack into an extendible arm that will move forward and back using the forward and reverse position on the drill. If you try it at this point, the steel tube will just spin and not extend and probably catch on your pantleg and leave you standing in the garage in your underwear. Again.

Once we add the other attachments to the tube, there will be enough weight and friction to add inertia, which will prevent the tube from moving.

Time now to move on to rotation. Once the arm is extended, we want to be able to rotate it 360 degrees in any direction. Well, actually, 360 degrees is *every* direction, so I guess I said that wrong.

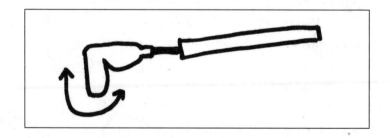

No wait, we need two planes of rotation and they have to be 90 degrees from each other. I think it's called a gimbal mount. It's kind of like the earth, if the earth could spin north-south in addition to east-west. I'm starting to get a headache. The good news is the first rotation is easy. All we need to do is twist the drill.

For the other rotation, which I'll call side to side, I suggest you take a close look at your tape measure. You're going to have to use your imagination, and I know you hate that, but when you pull out the tape, you can almost picture the spool turning inside the cover, and you'll also feel the force of a spring inside ready to wind the tape up again as soon as you let go. Those are exactly the conditions of motion that we need. Now, I'm not suggesting you wreck a perfectly good twelve-foot tape measure just to make a Canadarm, but maybe you know somebody who would lend you one. Mount the guts of the tape measure onto the side of a broomstick.

That will become the second leg of your arm. However, we need to allow the tape to move as the first arm is extended. This will require a second tape measure mounted on the drill. The

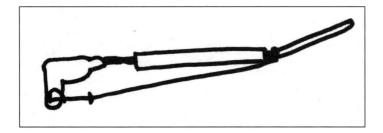

ends of the two tape measures will be connected. That way, as the arm extends and contracts, the tape will maintain its position.

(The second tape measure will not be damaged, so you can use your own.)

Now we're ready to move on to the pincers. Follow an old farmer home, and while he and his wife are watching *Wheel of Fortune*, sneak inside his barn and swipe his old ice tongs.

Wrap a bungee cord around the handles and attach the tongs to the other end of the broomstick.

Using the Handyman's Secret Weapon, duct tape, mount a fishing reel onto the side of the cordless drill.

Put a few screw eyes into the broomstick and run line from the fishing reel up through the screw eyes and tie the line to one of the ice-tong handles.

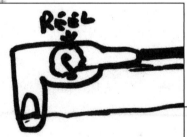

And it's just that easy. To test your new Canadarm, try to get an orange out of the fruit bowl on the kitchen table without leaving your seat in the living room.

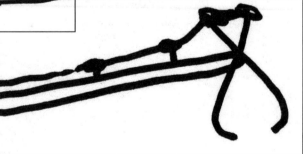

Rest the Canadarm on a chair to take the weight, and then point it at the fruit bowl. Use the drill to extend the house jack until the ice tongs are lined up with fruit bowl. (Notice how the tape measures adapt to the extension.) Turn the drill so that the approach angle is correct. Pull on the tape until the tongs surround the orange in question.

Use the fishing reel to close the ice tongs and pick up the orange. Now simply reverse the process to bring the orange back to you. When you unlock the reel, the bungee will cause the ice tongs to open and drop the orange into your lap. Nice work, commander.

To see how I used a Canadarm to take out the garbage, go to the Book of Inventions page at redgreen.com and click on "Canadarm."

CARBIDE ACETYLENE
Thomas "Carbide" Willson

Thomas Willson was born near Woodstock, Ontario, in 1860, and grew up to be the Canadian equivalent of Nikola Tesla, except he didn't get a car named after him. By the time Tom was twenty, he and a blacksmith buddy had built one of Canada's first electric dynamos and used it to give Hamilton electric arc lights. I guess that makes them the first dynamic duo?

And Thomas was just getting started. Next he went to the States and started his own electric company, but his biggest claim to fame was coming up with a better way to make acetylene. People were using acetylene as fuel in lights because it gave a strong, white light, especially when it exploded. But acetylene was complicated to make, so it was expensive.

Our pal Mr. Willson fixed all that when he figured out that all you had to do was add water to carbide and you'd get acetylene. That's how he got the nickname "Carbide." That was a lot better than the other suggestion—"Acetylene Legs."

Tom's process made acetylene a commercial success, and it led to the use of oxyacetylene welding, which is responsible for big buildings and bridges not falling down, which is always a good thing.

As a sideline, Carbide Willson adapted navigation buoys to have lights, powered by acetylene, that lasted way longer and shone way brighter than the old kerosene versions—and way, *way* brighter than the ones that just used scented candles.

✳ ✳ ✳

Thomas strikes me as a pretty sharp guy. And a pretty brave guy. Fooling around with electricity and acetylene is not for the faint of heart. And this was early days, when nobody really knew what they were doing. Like in the '50s, when we used to play catch with balls of uranium.

But Thomas figured out how it worked and then made it work for him by making it work for us. And while he was doing it, he was hedging his bets. He was investing in electricity, which he thought would eventually supply all of our lighting needs, but at the same time he was making a better fuel in case Plan A blew a fuse.

Definitely a smart guy and a pioneer. And of all of his creations, I gotta say the navigation buoy with the bright light is my favourite. If I'm out in a boat at night during a storm, the navigation buoy can't be bright enough, as far as I'm concerned. Who needs a navigation buoy that you can't see? It's just something else to hit. On the other hand, if I'm going to hit a buoy, I'd rather hit one that wasn't full of acetylene. So it's a double-edged sword.

Now, I know the world doesn't use acetylene for navigation buoys anymore and electricity has come a long way from Willson's early dynamo, but once in a while it's good to stop and pay some respect to what got you here. So give a little gratitude to Thomas "Carbide" Willson. And call your mother.

CARDIAC PACEMAKER
John Hopps

John Hopps was born in Winnipeg on May 21, 1919. He was pretty good in school and got his engineering degree from the University of Manitoba in 1941. He decided to do research work at the Banting Institute at the University of Toronto, where he started working on the effects of radio technology to warm up people suffering from hypothermia. I guess it was an early form of microwaving them.

But while he was trying different things, Hopps noticed that electrical impulses could get a stopped heart beating again. It was good news for dead people but a major setback for the electric chair. Eventually, John's team came up with the first-ever cardiac pacemaker in 1951. The unit was bigger than a kitchen table and plugged into a wall socket. For the portable unit, the kitchen table had casters and an extension cord. But this baby paved the way for internal pacemakers, which came along over the next ten years.

Canadian Wilson Greatbatch was a key player in the development of the internal pacemaker when he started using mercury batteries to run them. This allowed people with heart conditions to jog. For a little while.

This invention should almost have its own category. It has a pretty basic job—it keeps your heart beating. How important is that? I'm not a doctor, but I would say pretty important.

We all have a bunch of organs. Some are useful, some are just for show, some are vital. Vital is from the Latin word *vita*, which means "life." The vital organs are the ones that keep you alive. And the most vital of the vital is the heart. You can be brain-dead and still survive, but when you're heart-dead, you're *dead* dead.

In fact, being brain-dead is an asset for many jobs. Being heart-dead is only good news for the undertaker, and maybe some high-priced lawyers.

The pacemaker is the best friend your heart ever had. It's like jumper cables, training wheels, a safety net, a life jacket, a backup generator and life insurance for your heart. And it's so simple. They just lift a little skin and plug the darn thing in. And it's very reliable. In fact, it comes with a lifetime guarantee.

Come to think of it, that's pretty meaningless. But a pacemaker is so reliable, it often outlives the heart it's helping. And get this: they make you give it back. As if dying wasn't humiliating enough. But I guess if it can help somebody else, why not?

Personally, if I ever needed a pacemaker, I'd go brand new. Saving a couple of bucks on a reconditioned unit doesn't sound all that appealing. A few years ago, a guy at the Lodge got a real deal on a pacemaker through a friend of a friend of a really annoying guy. Two days after installation, he found out it was just a small alarm clock. The good news was he could now plan his heart attacks in advance by setting the alarm, but overall, not a good decision.

Other than that, I have nothing but good things to say about the cardiac pacemaker. In fact, they are now so easy to install that—in Ontario, at least—if you have any kind of a heart attack, the first thing they do is slap a pacemaker on ya. They do it in the ambulance while they're doing eighty clicks with the siren blaring. They just stick it on the outside of your chest, but it still works. One day in the future, you may be able to get it done at a hospital drive-thru, or maybe they'll cut out the middleman and just include them in every burger carton, like a Happy Meal toy.

The idea of the battery worries me, though. The battery is supposed to last a year, and you have to go back to the hospital to get a new one. So before you commit to a particular cardiologist, I would suggest you go over to his house and ask to go into his garage or his basement, wherever he keeps his tools.

Once you get there, look around in the bottom of his toolbox or in the back of a workbench drawer until you find an old, abandoned flashlight. Hold it up in front of your eyes and turn it on. You want it to temporarily blind you. If it's just bright but not annoying, or if it's a little dim—or worst of all, if it doesn't even go on—this is not the doctor for you. You don't want a guy who's casual about replacing batteries.

He may argue that he has a brand new flashlight on top of the workbench with fresh batteries in it, but you have been called a useless tool enough times to know that as a patient, you're in the back of one of the drawers.

Now that they've pretty much perfected the pacemaker in terms of size and reliability, isn't it time to take it up a notch? If I can put a dimmer on a light bulb, surely one of these medical researchers could find a way to add some kind of remote-control fader that would allow a person to control the pace of their pacemaker. I think it would be useful to be able to turn up the juice when you need it. Like during a foot race. Or lifting a fridge. Or that often-difficult wedding night of your sixth marriage. It would also be good to turn it down to a slow idle when you're trying to get to sleep. Or attending a family get-together. Or letting your wife drive.

If you have a life like mine, you could even add a timer that got you to sleep on time and gave you a kick-start in the morning. I would caution you, though, to make sure you keep the remote either on your person or in a secret hiding place. Once your wife gets her hands on it, you're a dead man. Literally.

If you'd like to see how I made a pacemaker, go to the Book of Inventions page at redgreen.com and click on "Pacemaker."

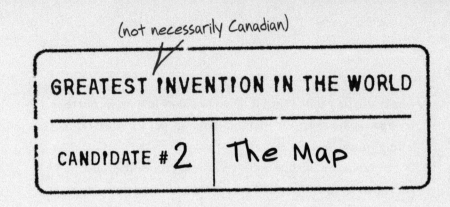

Maps have been around for thousands of years. The first maps were of the stars, which is weird because way back then nobody was planning to ever go there. But I guess it was a way of comparing the night sky to a drawing, and if the stars were all in the right place, so were you.

They've actually found these kinds of maps from about eighteen thousand years ago. And they still weren't folded properly.

Eventually people stopped just lying on the ground, staring at the sky, and instead started to move around. This was the beginning of the "paid vacation." The trouble with travelling was that nobody had a clue where they were going, which bothered a lot of the wives.

This created a job for the map-makers, who up until then had been universally unemployed. They were actually called cartographers, and they started making maps of the world around them so people could travel by land or sea without getting lost, or at least not *as* lost.

Maps started turning up independently all over the world. Some were small maps of a farm or a village. Others were of large areas, like provinces or countries. As the folks travelling with these maps bumped into each other at service centres, they were able to put the maps together and eventually have a map of the world. There were a few errors here and there, but it was certainly better than nothing, and maps got a lot more user-friendly when the cartographers all agreed to make north up, which led to the classic question, "What's up?" and the classic answer, "North."

Even as maps got better, it was still somebody's best guess as to what the continents and oceans looked like until we were able to go out into space and take pictures of the actual shape and size of everything on this funny little planet of ours.

RATING: A fine effort, but I'm sorry, no. Watch for Candidate #3, coming very soon to a book near you.

CAULKING GUN
Thomas Witte

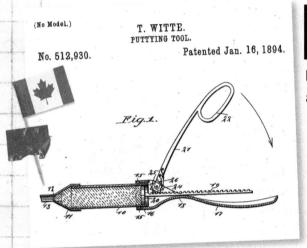

T. WITTE.
PUTTYING TOOL.

No. 512,930.

Patented Jan. 16, 1894.

Fig.1.

First Caulking Gun

Here's a Canadian inventor who really was under the radar. His name is Thomas Witte, and in 1894 he invented the caulking gun. We know that much. They say he had been inspired by local cake decorators and the tool they used to put icing on cakes. Witte's cakes didn't taste very good, but they lasted for months and were completely waterproof. Unfortunately, his invention was ahead of its time, and it wasn't until some years later that it caught on. Maybe if he'd waited until somebody invented caulking.

Yet another example of the brilliance of repurposing rather than starting from scratch. My guess is that the engineering for the cake decorator was pretty much identical to the engineering for the caulking gun—or "puttying tool," as Mr. Witte called it. And although I give him credit for stealing a good idea and avoiding all the cost and frustration of product development, the same lack of imagination that prevented him from creating a truly new invention also kept him from success. It was the name. Maybe the worst name ever. The name *hammer* sounds like something powerful and persistent. Even the word *screwdriver* has an aggressive edge to it. But "putting tool"? Tommy, Tommy, Tommy, if you weren't so Canadian, you would have realized that every man secretly loves the word *gun*. Add the word *gun* to anything and you have a hit: staple gun, nail gun, glue gun, heat gun, potato gun, cap gun, pop gun, water gun, Peter Gunn.

If they had invented a sunscreen gun, no man would ever have a sunburn. Which statement sounds more manly to you: "I will bring my putting tool" or "I'll be packin' my caulking gun"? Even if Thomas felt the word *caulking* was a little vulgar, he could have gone with "putting gun." But putting *tool*? No, Tom, it ain't happenin'.

So what should have been an instant success languished in the shadows for years until some hairy-chested plumber declared, "This ain't no putting tool, this here is a caulking gun." And suddenly every joint in town became safer.

✳ ✳ ✳

As with many inventions, there is a dark side to the caulking gun. It has to do with finding a way to make a decrease in the quality of workmanship an acceptable option.

In the early days of civilization, men did not have the tools or the talent to make anything other than crude artifacts. (Crude artifacts are still being made today, but mostly of rubber.) As time passed, men got better skills and better tools, and a number of them began to strive for perfection. During this period, many of the world's great buildings and furnishings were made. There was tremendous attention to detail, and patience was a virtue rather than an annoying delay. It was the birth of the craftsman. When he made something that was to be inserted into a hole, if it was too big, he'd methodically trim it down a few thousandths of an inch at a time until it was a perfect fit. If it was too small, he'd throw it away and start over. Very expensive, but quality never comes cheap.

With the invention of caulking—and, more importantly, the caulking gun—craftsmanship went out the window. It was much more cost-effective to make the thing too small from the get-go and then fill the gap with caulking. Or duct tape. We've now come to the era where it's better to do ten things okay than to do one thing well.

On a completely unrelated matter, the early 1950s found Stanley Barber in financial difficulty.

An entrepreneur by choice, but lazy by nature and not particularly bright by any means, Stanley ran the local bakery in Possum Lake. The business was failing, but Stanley hung on desperately, as the store had been in his family for almost seven

months. Stanley had tried everything. He went through a series of store name changes, including Muffin Tops, Great Danishes and even McDonuts, but nothing worked.

At one point he contemplated changing his own name because he thought a man named Barber running a bakery was confusing to the locals and made them wary of finding a hair in their apple turnover.

Not knowing which way to turn, Stan turned up an alley when something struck him. It was a potato. A friend from Stan's War of 1812 re-enactment club had built a potato gun to help celebrate St. Patrick's Day. He had been testing it for about an hour in the alley

Stanley Barber, Lodge Member, War of 1812 Re-enactment Guy

and was refining how far and how accurately it would shoot. His comfort level had risen to the point that he would shout out, "Do you want fries with that?" before firing a potato into the abyss.

Stanley was immediately excited about the concept and design of the potato gun, and once he regained consciousness, he began working on his own version of the weapon.

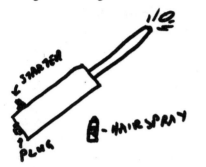

A potato gun is made from different diameters of PVC pipe all glued together, with a barbecue starter mounted on the side of the combustion chamber and a plug at the end. So you likely won't find it at Toys "R" Us. For those of you who've lived sheltered lives and don't know how a potato gun works, you sharpen the end of the barrel, which you then use to cut the potato so it fits snugly inside. Next, you unscrew the plug, squirt in some aerosol hairspray, replace the plug, aim the gun and hit the barbecue starter. *Blam!* That's what I call a spud missile.

Stan's plan was to adapt the gun so that instead of potatoes it would fire raisin-bran muffins. His thinking, if you can call it that, was that his bakery was failing because nobody went into it. His solution was to bring the product to the customer. At high speed, and with just a hint of Alberto VO5. Stan figured he could just fire the bran muffins into open bathroom windows if people had been in there too long. Once he built the gun, he spent days figuring out all the variables that would allow him to deliver the muffins to the right customer. His calculations involved the weight of the muffin, the angle of the barrel, the amount of hairspray and the number of raisins.

Sadly, Stanley had used the rent money to fund the muffin gun, and he was subsequently evicted from the store. He was unfazed because with his new delivery technique he could sell muffins from anywhere.

But apparently not *his* muffins. Stan closed down the business and went back to War of 1812 re-enactments, where he won several battles using only his wits and his muffin gun. Mainly his muffin gun.

RED SAYS: When working with large electrical coils, be careful not to magnetize your fly. Nobody wants to see you walk into church with a large pipe wrench hanging from the front of your pants.

CRISPY CRUNCH
Harold Oswin

Crispy Crunch—How Sweet It Is

C an you imagine a better job for an inventor than to be able to create new chocolate bars? I mean, other than the downside of weighing four hundred pounds and losing all your teeth, it would be like being at a birthday party every day.

Well, in the early 1900s, there was this guy named Harold Oswin, who started working as a candy roller for Neilson's in Toronto when he was fourteen years old. By the late '20s, he had moved all the way up the corporate ladder to candy maker. How good does that look on a resumé? Harold had always dreamed of making a candy that combined chocolate and peanut butter, and he got his chance when the company had a chocolate bar contest. Harold won and received the five-dollar prize. With this windfall he was now able to buy . . . several of his own candy bars.

Harold's chocolate bar was in the shape of a small brown log, but that's an image that often has a negative impact, so the company flattened it out into a slab. Crispy Crunch was a fairly popular chocolate bar from the get-go, but it really hit its stride in 1988 when the Leo Burnett advertising agency came up with the slogan "The only thing better than *your* Crispy Crunch is someone else's." That appealed to the thief in all of us, and Crispy Crunch went from being number ten to number one on the Canadian chocolate bar hit parade.

In the 1990s, Crispy Crunch was sold into the U.S., but the distributor went bankrupt and that was the end of that. At the same time, Neilson's tried out a lower-calorie version of the Crispy Crunch, which worked about as well as you would expect it to. In 1996, Neilson's sold all of its chocolate brands to Cadbury, which still makes the Crispy Crunch bar. It's a little sweeter and less salty than the original version and has a little more crunch because they took the candy coating up a notch.

* * *

I know a lot of people go for fortune and fame, but for me personally, there have gotta be a lot of good things about being in the chocolate-making business. For starters, you are instantly the favourite relative of every kid in your family and the favourite neighbour of every kid on your street. In most factories, when you make a mistake, you can't hide it. With chocolate, you can eat it. And women love chocolate. Your wife's never gonna be mad when you bring your work home with you. Plus, it's a great way to get on your dentist's good side, which will pay huge dividends when it's pain management time for your root canal.

Okay, I guess there are a couple of drawbacks—you take a lot of blame from mothers of fat kids with pimples, and the Easter

Bunny sees you as an enabler. But overall, you make people happy, and that's gotta feel good. The only thing that puzzles me about the Crispy Crunch story is why it didn't catch on in the U.S. I can't imagine anyone not liking a Crispy Crunch bar. Maybe it was too expensive to ship, or maybe a lot of Americans have a peanut allergy, or maybe they have developed different taste buds than us after years of drinking really weak beer. Either way, nice to know we've been able to keep some of our great ideas to ourselves.

THE CURE

Dr. Ralph Cosgrove, Lodge Doctor

In 1923, Lodge member and local physician Dr. Ralph Cosgrove discovered a cure for which there was no known disease.

At his request, Possum Lake Hospital has put six cases of his cure on ice in hopes of one day finding its true use. While no one will go on record, a few nurses admitted, after several drinks at a local pub, that some of the more daring employees will occasionally thaw out a vial to "tie on a Cosgrove."

Reports indicate that no medical effects have been detected, but the stuff tastes like peach schnapps mixed with Windex.

EASY-OFF OVEN CLEANER
Herbert McCool

Easy-Off oven cleaner was invented by Herbert McCool in 1932. Even though this was during the Great Depression, it's hard to imagine a man being so depressed that he started cleaning the oven. McCool was actually an electrician who lived in Regina, Saskatchewan. If he had been a chemist, he probably would never have come up with the concept of using a volatile acid to etch the goo off your oven racks. He made the product in his basement and sold it door to door until his death in 1946. His widow later sold the rights for the oven cleaner to American Home Products and Boyle Midway Canada.

✳ ✳ ✳

For me, the beauty of this product is that ole Herb came up with a formula that was strong enough to clean an oven but safe enough to have in your kitchen. If I had invented it, it would be made out of sulphuric acid and come in a huge can so they had room to print all the warnings. If there's one thing that's more dangerous than acid, it's gotta be acid in an aerosol can. My slogan would be "It gets rid of grease *and* the ozone layer in one easy spray!" No woman would pay twenty dollars for mace when all she needs is a can of my oven cleaner. But that's the difference between McCool and me. He knew things and he did tests until he came up with the perfect balance between safety and getting the job done. I tend to focus on getting the job done.

Nobody enjoys cleaning ovens. Nobody enjoys cleaning toilets either, but at least the stuff's not baked on.

So here I'd come with my nuclear-grade oven cleaner. It'd be similar to Easy-Off. You'd just spray it on and let it sit and then it wipe off. Sure, there'd be a few drawbacks, like having to wear welding gloves to use my formula, and a little over-spray in the wrong direction potentially costing you an eye. And for the next week or so, all the pies would come out of the oven tasting like coal.

So I guess making oven cleaner is just one more line of work I was smart not to get into.

Sid Pagano, Fearless Dabbler

Local resident Sid Pagano regarded Easy-Off as the starting point for an almost limitless number of similar products that worked in the same way but were just different enough to avoid lawsuits. His approach was simple: take random mixtures of a bunch of chemicals and then package them in brightly coloured, playful pressurized cans. He tried marketing a bee repellant called Buzz-Off, an airplane de-icer called Take-Off and a front-door restorer he called Knock-Off. The local reaction was overwhelming but not positive.

Our chamber of commerce started calling Sid's business Way-Off and eventually forced him to leave town, which they called a Send-Off. Sid was fine. He labelled it a Write-Off.

WARNING: There are a few different areas of science represented in this book, but this invention falls squarely in the chemistry category. A lot of people these days aren't sure whether chemistry is a good thing or a bad thing. One of the big chemical companies used the slogan "Better Living Through Chemistry," but some folks say that what's better for one person is sometimes worse for another. They would prefer the slogan "*Longer* Living Through Chemistry," which may be a tougher challenge.

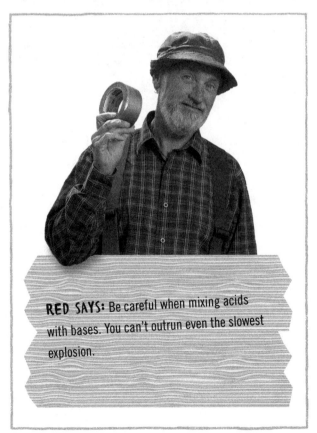

RED SAYS: Be careful when mixing acids with bases. You can't outrun even the slowest explosion.

EGG CARTON
Joseph Coyle

The egg carton was invented in 1911. This was thousands of years after the invention of the scrambled egg. The world has always been full of slow learners.

The inventor of the egg carton was a newspaper editor named Joseph Coyle of Smithers, British Columbia. He did it to solve an argument between a local farmer and a hotel owner in the area. The disagreement was over the farmer's eggs often being delivered broken and who should take the blame. My guess is that the hotel guy didn't want to pay for broken eggs, which meant the farmer wasn't able to afford his newspaper subscription. In walks Mr. Coyle and everybody wins.

✳ ✳ ✳

I'm sure it was a big help to the entire egg industry to have a new form of packaging that cut down on the amount of breakage. Up to that point, eggs were transported in an egg basket.

Not the smartest way to carry eggs during a time of cobblestone roads and wooden-wheeled wagons. A practice that required a general lack of respect for things like gravity. That led to the popular expression "Don't put all your eggs in one basket." But as you can see from the picture, you'd have to have a very low egg inventory to be able to get them all in one basket.

Egg Basket

So the egg carton not only made the eggs safer, it increased the minimum number of eggs the customer had to buy at one time. Generally sold in dozens (although the carton in the picture only holds ten—a metric dozen, maybe?), the farmer could get more egg sales per buyer. The days of the one-egg, or the dreaded half-egg, sales were over.

But the more practical use of the egg carton was discovered by local Possum Lake resident Beatrice Schmomf. Known to residents as Bea Schmomf (which was also her motto), she recognized the egg carton as a light, compact, yet pretty strong storage container for small pieces of jewellery or craft supplies or sewing machine bobbins or individual teeth. She made her own clothes, as you can see from the nautical outfit she's wearing on page 62, but was unsuccessful in persuading any major fashion house to get on board.

Beatrice Schmomf, Craft Queen and Man Hater

Bea had a minimal social life and instead turned to crafts as her life partner. She took up sewing and needlework and pottery and embroidery and zentangles and stained glass and watercolours and basket weaving and crocheting and quilting and solitaire and welding. Each of these crafts needed a supply of raw materials, usually made up of a whole bunch of small pieces that gave her an infinite number of possible combinations.

Having all those options at her fingertips meant a person could have a tea cozy for every day of the week. Or as Bea would say, "Every day of the *year*!" After which she'd go into her huge, snorty laugh that always ended with a crying jag that often lasted more than an hour.

In her later years, Bea became very bitter. She stayed alone in her house with her crafts and rejected any contact with the outside world. She was over halfway through a giant, eight-foot needlepoint that said, "Drop Dead" when, ironically, she did. As the authorities searched her home, they found over twelve thousand egg cartons and her will, which asked that her body be laid out on top of the stacked cartons in the form of a raft that was to be set on fire and floated out to sea.

Her wishes were carried out, and that is how Beatrice Schmomf left us. That was her eggsit. I can almost hear that snorty laugh.

This should be an eye-opener for you budding inventors out there. If you can't think of anything new to invent, find some-thing that's already out there and invent a better holder for it. And the egg carton is not the only example in this book. Check out the jockstrap and the Wonderbra—same principle.

There is no shame in inventing something that makes something else better. In fact, I would say that the holder is often as important as the item itself. For example, a holster. Can you imagine the Lone Ranger galloping across the plains with a six-gun in each of his pants pockets? Or a quiver. General Custer would have been fine if the Plains Indians had had to carry their extra arrows in their teeth.

So take a look around and see if you can find something that would be better if it had some kind of decent holder. But please don't crochet any more toilet-paper cozies.

RED SAYS: When hammering large nails, hold them with the fingers you use least.

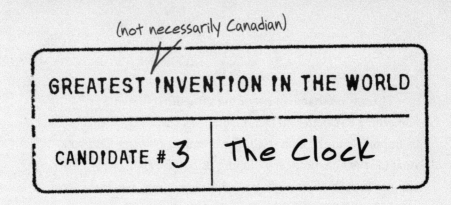

The purpose of a clock is to tell, and keep telling accurately, the current time in the zone where the clock is operating. The clock started out as a pretty simple machine, but as more and more men got involved, it got so complicated it'd give you a headache.

Probably the simplest version was the sundial, which told time using the shadow cast by the sun as it moved through the sky. The technology wasn't so great, but the best part was that on a cloudy day, nobody could tell if you were late for work. And any appointments after sundown were a crapshoot.

Actually, lots of different things have been used to tell time over the years. Moving beads of water or sand in a glass, or incoming tides, but the most consistently reliable way is by using moms. My mother always knew when it was time for dinner, time for a bath, time for bed, and, unfortunately, even when it was time for a talking-to.

Women have internal clocks. They start ticking loudly when that woman wants to have a baby, or when a nearby man says or does something inappropriate, or as soon as leftover chocolate cake gets put in the fridge. Those kinds of clocks are nearly impossible to understand, unless you are either a mind reader or even remotely paying attention, so I say it's better to use a digital one. Or analog if you are a bit of a show-off.

But whatever type of clock you like, you gotta admit it's been a pretty useful invention over the years. Without clocks, we'd never know how late we are.

RATING: Better than a calendar, but still not the greatest invention in the world of all time ever. Candidate #4 coming up next.

ELECTRIC OVEN
Thomas Ahearn

Thomas Ahearn was born in Ottawa on June 24, 1855. If there was ever a guy who deserved the nickname Sparky, Tommy boy is it. A pioneer in the field of electricity and its implementations, Thomas brought streetcars to Ottawa. He then had the patent filed for the first electric car heater and the first electric oven in 1892. When you live in Ottawa, you like things that generate heat.

Later that year, he cooked up an elaborate meal for a party of fifty (which he delivered by streetcar), using only his electric oven—the first meal of its kind ever recorded. Pretty impressive when you invent how a meal is cooked *and* the vehicle that delivers it.

✳ ✳ ✳

In school, we were taught that electricity is kind of like water. It flows. And if you've got a big lake at one end of a river and a little pond at the other, the water will go from the big one to the little one. Electricity does the same thing, but inside a wire instead of a river. But water will not go uphill without a pump. Electricity goes wherever it wants without anything. And water has a way of changing and adapting to whatever obstacles it comes up against. If the riverbed isn't wide enough to handle all the water that's going by, the water just flows up over the sides and through a bunch of basements.

If the wire isn't thick enough to handle all the electricity that's going by, the electricity has nowhere else to go, so it just keeps hammering through the wire, smashing into molecules, which generates enough heat to eventually melt the wire, which breaks the connection, causing the electricity to go nuts because it has to go *somewhere*, so it starts arcing wildly in all directions until it senses someone nearby who has a metal plate in their head and bare feet.

Water would never do that. So I would say electricity is different from water. In the same way that a nuclear warhead is different from a party balloon.

It's not really a shock that Mr. Ahearn worked with streetcars before he invented the electric oven. They're both machines that harness the energy from electricity and convert it into a more useful and controllable form. The streetcar converts the electricity to magnetism that makes a motor turn, which moves the streetcar. The oven converts the electricity to heat. With both of them, the key ingredient is a supply of consistent, regulated electricity.

The voltage and available amperage of direct current is supplied evenly to the streetcar motor. That's what makes it manageable. You couldn't do that with a lightning bolt. The result would be more of a streetcar dragster. Same thing with the oven—a steady supply of alternating current converts to a steady supply of heat and prevents the owner from fluctuating between cold soup and a kitchen fire.

But of the two, the oven is the most scientific. That's because of the need to match the components. It's all about resistance. It's like a marriage—if there's too much resistance, everything shuts down. But if there's no resistance, there's no heat—not even the good kind.

So once you've got your steady supply of regulated electricity, the burner becomes the next important piece of the puzzle. That's because every element in nature has its own resistance to electric current. Copper has almost none. Electricity whips through copper like swine flu through a cruise ship. But try getting electricity to go through a rock sometime. I would say trees are more or less the middle ground. Nowhere near as good a conductor as copper, but it's still possible to get electricity through a tree, as many lightning bolts have discovered.

So my guess is that Mr. Ahearn's biggest breakthrough with the electric oven was finding the right metal formulation for the burners. Something that would have enough resistance to heat up but not burn out. Without those elements, you got no elements.

The real danger with electricity again, like a marriage, is that after a while you take it for granted. And then you're in for a shock. The average house these days has a box in the basement that distributes 220 volts of electricity at 100 amps or more. That's a lotta juice. And if you don't believe me, try plugging a bobby pin into an electrical outlet. Actually please, *please* don't try that.

You've got all kind of things in your house that convert electricity to a usable form. Like streetcars, you've got a bunch of electromagnetic motors in your house—ceiling fans, furnace blowers, refrigerator and air conditioning compressors, garage door openers, blenders, power tools, etc. And other stuff that converts electricity to heat—ovens, toasters, baseboard heaters, light bulbs, etc.

And in the last fifty years or so we've found a way to use electricity as electricity—TVs, computers, security cameras, etc. Okay, that's all good, but we don't want to ever take electricity for granted. Print these rules off and hang them at eye height:

- Never dry your hair while taking a bath.
- Do not sit on a stove, even if triple-dog dared to.
- Don't wear your Abe Lincoln hat if there's a ceiling fan.
- If a breaker keeps tripping, don't try to glue it in the ON position.
- If you do your own wiring, go the extra mile and connect the ground wire. Otherwise you'll come home late one night, flip on the porch light and the electricity will arc out of the switch and nail the car keys hammocked in your pants pocket.
- Don't go near anything that's humming and smoking. Especially if it's your uncle.

Regardless of where our electricity comes from—waterfalls, solar or wind—I think it's going to be a bigger part of our lives in the future.

I've got all kinds of ideas for experiments that could be done to improve the human experience. Okay, maybe not all kinds. But certainly one kind. For example, we all learned at an early age that you can create a magnetic field by wrapping wire around a toilet paper roll and then hooking it up to a battery. And if you slipped it over a metal rod, the rod became a magnet. The opposite also worked: if you slipped a magnetic rod into a toilet paper roll wrapped in wire, you'd generate electricity.

Why can't we try that on a bigger scale? Build an experimental house, and instead of the wiring just going randomly through the walls, have it all go in windings through the perimeter.

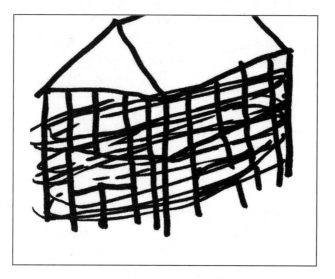

Now you would actually live inside a magnetic field. What would that do? Would magnetic people be more focused? Taller? Polish? For sure they'd be more attractive. And after a few years of building their magnetism, they'd be able to go off the grid by jumping up and down and generating their own electricity. What can I say? It's a gift.

To see a gigundo oven that I made, go to the Book of Inventions page at redgreen.com and click on "Oven."

AN EXPERIMENTAL MEDICATION

Willy Flann

In a desperate attempt to self-medicate without first getting the advice of a medical doctor, local dance instructor Willy Flann proved once and for all that hemorrhoids should never be treated with cayenne pepper.

THE FIRST DOCUMENTARY

The truest and most human story of the Great White Snows

A picture with more drama, greater thrill, and stronger action than any picture you ever saw.

REVILLON FRÈRES
PRESENT

NANOOK OF THE NORTH

A STORY OF LIFE AND LOVE IN THE ACTUAL ARCTIC

PRODUCED BY
ROBERT J. FLAHERTY, F.R.G.S.

Pathépicture

It fudged the facts a little

When it came out in 1922, *Nanook of the North* was the first-ever full-length documentary. The movie showed the struggles of an Inuk guy named Nanook and his family as they travelled across northern Quebec, looking for food and making trades. This later became known as "shopping."

There was a little brouhaha over portions of the film that were criticized for being staged, including Nanook's wives actually being filmmaker Roger Flaherty's common-law wives, and the Inuit hunting with spears instead of the guns they usually used.

Talk about nitpicking. It's not like this is a movie that anybody actually watched. Despite these hiccups, most people say the film is a testament to the heroism and accuracy of its characters. It was one of the first twenty-five films the Library of Congress chose to preserve for being "culturally, historically, or aesthetically significant." It's an honour, but it didn't make Flaherty rich. The box office returns from the Library of Congress have always been pretty disappointing.

✳ ✳ ✳

Based on the feelings of the guys I hang out with, my guess is that most people would never watch a documentary on purpose. They prefer big stories with lots of adventure and excitement and car explosions. Normal people like horror or sci-fi or just a guy with a chip on his shoulder and a really, really big gun. But what's weird is that these same people watch reality television. And why? Because it's not called "documentary." But it's the same thing. Showing people in their daily lives, getting into big arguments and having huge emotional breakdowns just before going to commercial.

And they're just as fake as Roger's Nanook movie. People only act naturally when they're alone. Even then, some of them have to turn off the lights. Have you ever seen what happens to people when you ask them to pose for a picture? A usually normal-looking human being turns into the Madame Tussaud's version of himself. You're trying to capture a memory and instead get a photo of someone you don't even recognize. That's because most people are naturally self-conscious. And the ones who aren't, should be.

And if they go all fake in front of a still camera, imagine how unnatural they are when a crew of fifty brings lights and cameras and a craft-service vehicle into their world. So Roger was right on the money when he fudged the facts a little. Some people like fake because it's entertaining. Others like true documentary because it feels real. But almost everybody likes fake documentary because it feels real *and* is entertaining.

Reality is almost never entertaining. Ask a proctologist.

———

Gladys Finch, Local Filmmaker
and Hat Collector

Inspired by Roger Flaherty's being okay with exaggerating and even altering the actual facts, Possum Lake's Gladys Finch decided to produce her own documentary on *The Effects of Celibacy on Man.* Using her husband, Walter, as the subject matter, she filmed the changes in his appearance and behaviour while she denied him any form of physical intimacy over a period of twenty years.

The unfortunate few who saw the film said it seemed a lot longer than the twenty years it took to make it.

It's a common mistake in the movie industry for a producer to have too much power during the editing process. Critics were unanimous in their verdict that many of the scenes should have been cut out of the film. Some said *all* of the scenes should have been cut out of the film.

The surprising part of the movie was the improvement in Walter's appearance, health and mood as he lived through the ordeal for all that time. After each year of celibacy, he was happier, more fit, ageless, mentally sharper and getting more and more involved with charitable work in the community. Based on the film, it was natural to figure that having a physically healthy relationship makes men miserable, fat, old, stupid and useless.

Gladys was very proud of her documentary and entered it in the Possum Lake Film Festival, where it won a prize for length. The film had a limited run at the Possum Lake Theatre. The duration of the limited run was three hours, which was around the halfway point. The last line of the movie, which almost nobody ever saw, was Walter looking straight into the camera and saying, "I did not have sexual relations with that woman."

Years later, Gladys would admit that although the documentary made a social statement, there was a little fakery going on. It was shot in twenty *weeks*, not years, and the big change in Walter's appearance and mood came at the three-week mark, when their divorce was finalized. Walter said later that the whole celibacy thing didn't apply to him being with other women.

To see how the Lodge was used for a documentary, go to the Book of Inventions page at redgreen.com and click on "Documentary."

RED SAYS: If you see explosives lying on a concrete floor, take off your tap shoes.

FIVE-PIN BOWLING
Thomas F. Ryan

Thomas F. Ryan was born in Guelph, Ontario, in 1872. He moved to Toronto at the age of eighteen, and fifteen years after, in 1905, he opened the Toronto Bowling Club. That makes sense—a thirty-two-year-old swinging guy in the big city lookin' for a little action, and step one is to open a bowling alley.

In 1909 he was getting complaints that the ten-pin ball was too heavy, so he switched to a lighter, hand-sized hard rubber ball. The smaller ball didn't have enough oomph or size to knock down ten large, heavy pins, so Ryan cut the number of pins in half, shaved them down in size, and five-pin bowling was invented. However, girls continued to be unattracted to guys with small balls and rented shoes.

✳ ✳ ✳

Although most of us in Canada have enjoyed five-pin bowling all these years, this story of how it all began is a little embarrassing. Modern ten-pin bowling started in New York in 1840, so the game had already been around for seventy years when suddenly a few bowlers from Toronto decided the ball was too heavy for them. Well, wah, wah, wah.

And what a message to send to our American friends—"We're not nearly as strong as you. We are pathetic." Lucky for us, the Americans weren't really listening. (Not that uncommon.) But what's worse, instead of telling the Canucks to suck it up, Ryan said, "Oh, okay . . . sorry . . . here, try this . . . and look, I've made the pins smaller. I can make them lean a little, if that would help . . ." This guy was obviously never in the Marines. And how about those wuss bowlers? Bowling was too hard?! We needed to make it easier?! Don't ever try golf.

Bowling may be a fun game, but it's gotta be a tough business to run. Look at the investment. You have to find a big building and put in all the bowling equipment, have a huge parking lot, buy bowling shoes for men, women, boys and girls in every possible size. And in five-pin, the players don't even bring their own balls. You can't have other tenants in the building. You're not gonna see a bank under a bowling alley.

Once you've moved in, you spend a fortune installing the wooden bowling alleys—which need to be perfectly level with a high-gloss finish. Then comes the worst part: the customers. You're forced to rent brand new bowling shoes to a big, fat sweaty guy with holes in his socks. He lights up a stogie, grabs the heaviest ball he can find and tosses it overhand in the general direction of the pins.

By the end of the night he's trashed the shoes and pounded dents into the alley. He pays his twelve dollars and leaves, and here's the worst part: you're hoping he comes back.

Local entrepreneur and ex–pin boy Frank Shortt was offended by the introduction of this new five-pin game he called "bawling," followed by Frank crying fake tears as he mocked the other

players. He decided to go the other way. He used to say, "Bowling is a man's game. It's not for sissies. If you can't stand the heat, take off your rented shoes." Frank loved everything about bowling— the smoke-filled air, the smell of the shoes, the sounds of heavy balls rolling and pins

Frank Shortt, Lodge Member and Alley Rat

getting smashed to the floor. Frank loved that bowling takes place in an alley, because rough things happen in alleys. To him, five-pin bowling belonged on the lawn of a daycare centre.

So Frank reacted by manning up. If you look closely at the picture above, you'll see that Frank is actually bowling with a forty-five-pound cannonball he stole from Old Fort York. How manly is that? But it still wasn't tough enough for Frank, so he took the ten-pin concept up a notch. He made it *one*-pin bowling.

It was one pin for each of ten frames, so it was still technically ten-pin bowling. It made the game more difficult, but the big plus was that when Frank hit a pin with the cannonball, it splintered into a million pieces. Frank loved that part. Sadly, Frank's version of the game never got off the ground—and neither, for most people, did the cannonball.

Bitter and alone, Frank would go to the lanes late at night and play his game all by himself in an end alley.

Rumours even circulated that he would challenge random bowlers to a "bowl duel," where the opposing player had to stand in as the pin. No one ever took Frank up on his offer. Within a year his spine collapsed from the stress of bowling, and he was forced to have back surgery. They put a pin in it.

And what would happen if the Ryan family tradition were to continue?

June 1, 2025—Today, Edgar Ryan, great-great-great-great-grandson of Thomas F. Ryan, the father of five-pin bowling, was appointed commissioner of the National Football League. Ed says changes will be coming.

February 1, 2026—In response to complaints from the players about the roughness of play and overall difficulty of the game, Commissioner Ryan has abolished blocking and tackling. You are permitted to stand in front of a player running with the ball, thereby viciously forcing him to go around you. As soon as the player with the ball is touched anywhere in the region of the buttocks by an opposing player, the play will be whistled dead.

October 1, 2026—Reacting to what the league office is calling an inordinate amount of buttock-region touching, Commissioner Ryan has adopted the rules of flag football, whereby the player with the ball has a flag attached loosely to his uniform—and nowhere near the buttock area—and play will be stopped when an opposing player removes that flag. When asked about attendance figures being down by over 80 per cent, the commissioner had no response.

February 15, 2027—Bad news for the Super Bowl. With fewer than one hundred tickets sold—all of them to employees of the company that made the flags—Commissioner Ryan is shutting down the league and turning it into a card game so that the fans who are not coming to the games can still enjoy the sport without anybody getting hurt. France declares football its new national sport.

To see Adventurer Bill try bowling, go to the Book of Inventions page at redgreen.com and click on "Bowling."

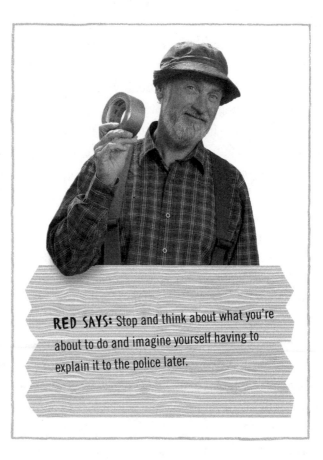

RED SAYS: Stop and think about what you're about to do and imagine yourself having to explain it to the police later.

FOGHORN
Robert Foulis

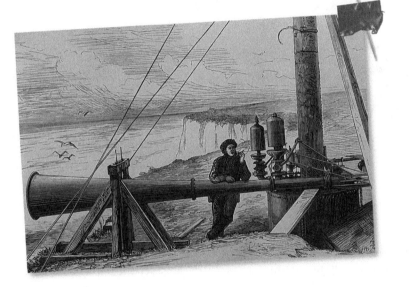

Robert Foulis was born in Scotland in 1796. He came to Canada in 1818, settling in Halifax, which is in Nova Scotia, which is Latin for "New Scotland," so he felt right at home—or at least would have if he had understood Latin. After a while, he moved to Saint John, New Brunswick. I guess he couldn't resist the lure of the big city.

In 1853, while taking a walk, he heard his daughter playing the piano and realized that, from a distance, only the low notes came through. Maybe he went for a walk every time his daughter started practising the piano—we'll never know. But on this occasion, it gave him the idea for the steam foghorn.

In 1859, the government gave Robert and his gang the go-ahead to build the first-ever steam foghorn on a spot called Partridge Island. Can you imagine the load of bird droppings the partridges released the first time somebody fired up the foghorn?

✳ ✳ ✳

 Not meaning to take anything away from Mr. Foulis, but the foghorn pretty much plays a second-banana role to the more popular and less annoying fog *light*. This is because the human senses are much better at figuring out where light is coming from than where sound is coming from. If humans were any good at identifying the sources of sounds, a lot of ventriloquists would be out of business and a lot fewer dogs would be blamed for that smell in the living room.

Sometimes when you're driving, you'll hear a siren, but you don't really know where it's coming from until you see the flashing lights on the roof of the car and see the cop get out and walk towards you. So, although the foghorn is a sort of useful bonus, if it were the only fog signal, the crews of ships at sea would be aware there was a big rock out there somewhere, just not exactly sure where. They'd have to stay perfectly still until the fog dissipated, which in Newfoundland can be months.

In the early 1900s, local entrepreneur and self-taught astrophysicist Douglas Bigelow used the results of Foulis's studies as the starting point for experiments on sound and how it travels. Mr. Bigelow, or "Dougie," as he was known to the local cops, discovered that in addition to the lowest frequencies of sound travelling the farthest, every frequency within the audible human spectrum has a distance at which it can no longer be heard.

Dougie began by having an assistant hold a high-pitched, shrill military whistle within an inch of his ear and then blow into it as hard as he could. (The whistle, not Dougie's ear.) The results were a valuable lesson for both of them. Dougie lost the hearing in his left ear for ten days, and his assistant's right eye was swollen shut for approximately the same length of time.

Douglas Bigelow, Lodge Member and Sound Thinker

As they carried on doing more experiments, they were able to figure out, within a few inches, how far a sound would travel based on its frequency, amplitude, air temperature, barometric pressure, humidity, wind speed, wind direction and surrounding sound levels. They sent in a report to the academic magazine *Scientifica Americana*, claiming that a sound with a frequency of 2,400 hertz and an amplitude of 97 decibels on a 70-degree (Fahrenheit) day with 15 millibars of air pressure, 37 per cent humidity, a 7-mile-per-hour southeasterly wind and virtually no measurable ambient noise levels would travel 507 feet before dropping out of the human hearing range. (Subject to how well that person could hear. For example, Moose Thompson can hear a dinner bell anywhere within a two-mile range, and Buster Hadfield can only hear his wife when she's calling from the bedroom.)

The magazine decided not to publish the article, saying it was unreliable, unscientific, had no practical application and was boring, even by their standards. Dougie and his assistant wouldn't hear of it. Instead they continued with their experiments until they ran out of funds, which was later that same week.

There's something about the invention of the foghorn that really points out how far technology has come. The basic premise of the foghorn, and other inventions like it, is that it is geared specifically to increase the range and power of human senses. If we had better hearing, we wouldn't need a foghorn. We'd be able to hear the waves lapping up on shore and have a pretty good idea of how close we were getting.

Hundreds of years ago, inventors had no other choice but to gear their inventions to the limitations of human beings. IBM changed all that. These days, almost all of us are carrying a little device that can tell us exactly where we are and how to get where we're going. It's called a global positioning system, and it uses satellite signals instead of human ears.

Ultraviolet cameras are way better than human eyes. In fact, there are artificial detectors of everything from earth tremors to bad smells that are way more sensitive than any of our bodies.

The only thing we still have going for us is our brains, but the clock is ticking. Someday soon, the smartest person will be dumber than the dumbest computer. Some of us have a head start.

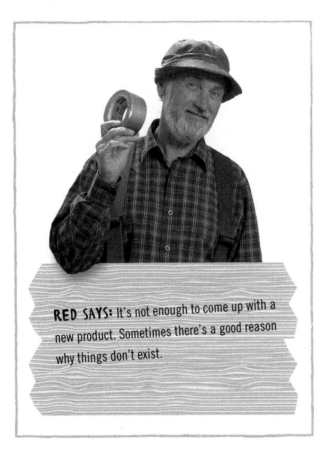

RED SAYS: It's not enough to come up with a new product. Sometimes there's a good reason why things don't exist.

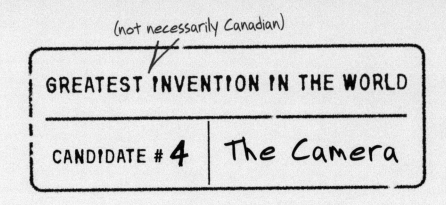

The first pinhole camera was invented in fourth-century China and was given the name "camera obscura" by the Europeans, who caught up with the idea a few centuries later.

They made excellent, sharp images. So far, so good. But until the invention of photography, it wasn't easy to capture that image. You had to project the picture onto a piece of paper or canvas and then trace it. And if you were a really bad tracer or had a couple of extra coffees in you, the tracing could end up worse than somebody with talent just drawing the picture from scratch. So the camera obscura fell into obscurity.

In the sixteenth century, Reinerus Gemma Frisius—a math guy from what's now the Netherlands—used the camera obscura to allow himself to watch a solar eclipse without going blind. So even though it couldn't take pictures, a camera obscura was still worth keeping handy for when an eclipse came around every hundred years or so.

Eventually, film came along, and that was really a turning point for cameras. But there was a drawback to be overcome: cameras were huge. That's because the size of the negatives determined the size of the picture, so if you wanted an eight-by-ten-inch photo, you needed an eight-by-ten negative. And controlling the light was a necessity. People would actually have to go into a room-sized apparatus to get their pictures taken by a gigundo camera.

The photographer would sometimes sing. "You've gotta accentuate the negative," but only if he'd been paid in advance.

Gradually, cameras got smaller and smaller, and the lenses got better and better, and Photoshop made us all look good.

RATING: Okay, we're getting closer, but we're still nowhere near the G.I.I.T.W.O.A.T.E. Watch for Candidate #5.

FOX 40
Ron Foxcroft

In 1987, Hamilton, Ontario, businessman and NCAA basketball referee Ron Foxcroft invented the Fox 40 Pealess Whistle. He was frustrated by the normal sports whistle, whose pea would jam and prevent a ref from calling fouls or stopping play or directing traffic.

Mr. Foxcroft developed the Fox 40, with some help from a design consultant named Chuck Shepherd, who I guess was a whistle specialist. They introduced their new whistle at the 1987 Pan American Games in Indianapolis. It immediately became the gold standard in sports whistles.

I think it took so long to improve on the whistle design because no one wanted to admit they were having trouble with their pea. Congratulations to Mr. Foxcroft, who got over that hurdle and found a way to make something better by making it simpler. Very rare. The horseless carriage pales when compared to the pealess whistle.

✳ ✳ ✳

Interestingly enough, local Possum Lake referee George Fistlewick was ruined by this same invention. George had long been suspected of miscalling local middle-school girls' basketball games to support a private gambling habit. In 1989, George was interviewed after a game where he missed calling twenty-seven fouls in a row. And they were all against the same team.

George claimed that the pea had stuck in his whistle, but unbeknownst to George, the school had switched to the Fox 40. George excused himself and went for a pea but it was too late. For the rest of the basketball season, the whistles remained pealess and the games remained Georgeless.

George Fistlewick

I'm not sure if you've noticed this, but in this book of Canadian inventions I've counted eleven that are some-how connected to a sport or a game. That's a pretty high percent-age from a country that's supposed to be a little on the serious side. The message I'm getting is that Canadians like to have their fun, and if you come up with an invention to make those things better, Canada will be there for you.

Yes, we've had our huge medical breakthroughs, like the cardiac pacemaker and insulin, but let's not forget the jockstrap and the pealess whistle. They've gotta be right up there. To me, it shows the range of the Canadian people. There may not be a lot of us, but we don't need a whole bunch of people to cover a lot of different areas. When you grow up in a country this big, you learn how to spread out.

FROZEN FOOD
A.G. Huntsman

Archibald G. Huntsman was born in Tintern, Ontario, in 1883. He was really good in academics, and after he got his medical degree at the University of Toronto, he decided to go into the field of marine biology. Today, that would probably sound fishy, but it was a different time.

From 1924 to 1928, Archie was the director of the Fisheries Experimental Station in Halifax, which is where he worked on a way to fast-freeze fish fillets. He called them "Ice Fillets" and started marketing them to the general public. It was going well, even without a catchy name or slogan or bouncy jingle, but the Canadian government had qualms about one of its own agencies competing with private companies who paid the taxes that funded the agencies that forced them to compete with themselves.

The frozen fish project was put on ice, but the technology was made available for any commercial business that was paying attention. I guess Archie wasn't the kind of guy to take an idea and run with it. Maybe when you work for the government, you don't *have* to be.

✳ ✳ ✳

Doesn't feel like much of a stretch to find out that frozen food was invented in a country that has nine months of winter. Anybody who's ever had a flat tire from driving over roadkill in February knows that it gets a little chilly north of the forty-ninth parallel.

Frozen food was not really a new concept. Any animal that doesn't hibernate spends most of the winter eating frozen food. The real breakthrough that Archie came up with was the ability to freeze things fast. Real fast. If you just throw a side of beef into a snowbank, yes, it will eventually freeze, but it picks up a lot of bacteria and germs and dry rot along the way. But if you had a big enough catapult, you could shoot it into outer space, where it would freeze in about twelve seconds.

That's what Mr. Huntsman figured out how to do. Not toss food into space, but get it cold at hyper speed.

It's actually just math. The amount of heat in anything can be calculated in BTUs (British thermal units). Let's say you're wondering how many BTUs are in a rump roast. First you weigh it, and then you take its temperature using a rectal thermometer. You multiply those numbers together and you get a number—let's say it's 500 BTUs. If you put the roast into a normal freezer, which is cold enough to absorb 100 BTUs an hour, it'll take five hours to freeze your butt.

But if you drop the roast into something really, really cold, like liquid nitrogen or the gaze of an upset wife, your rump will be frozen in six or seven seconds. You could almost say it's frozen in time. In fact, I almost said it.

And all thanks to Archie G. He started with fish, which was the least dense meat and easiest to freeze, but was enough to get the ice ball rolling. Just not for him. That's because the government wouldn't let him.

I know it says it was because the government had "qualms" about competing with private companies, but I don't think that was the reason. I think the government knew that if it commercialized the idea, it'd screw it up somehow. It'd have the usual fifteen people doing the job of two, and doing it badly, and getting huge salaries and a month's vacation along with all statutory and religious holidays off. Whereas actual businessmen would create an industry that was hugely successful, and therefore hugely taxable. The government wins either way, but taxation is really what it does best.

And this was just the beginning. Huntsman's frozen food created a few new industries. Grocery stores suddenly had to have huge freezer sections, which spawned an industrial freezer industry; and then people wanted freezers in their homes, which built a residential freezer industry; and then people started freezing their leftovers and storing them in freezer bags, which built a freezer bag industry—okay, not as big as the other two, but you get the idea.

And then freezers would break, which built a freezer-repairman industry that ultimately declined into a guy just telling you to buy a new freezer. And every person who worked in any of those industries paid taxes. So instead of the government investing in Huntsman's idea and creating a viable business of its own, it did nothing and it paid off huge.

You can't really blame the government for making "do nothing" its default position.

To see what I do with frozen food, go to the Book of Inventions page at redgreen.com and click on "Frozen."

GOALIE MASK
Jacques Plante

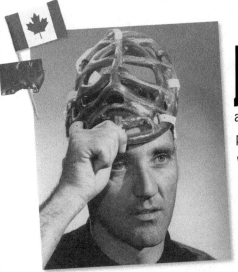

Jacques Plante, born in Quebec on January 17, 1929, was the first goalie to wear a full face mask in an NHL game. He started using it in practice, but his coach, Toe Blake, wouldn't let him use it in a game—which was weird, because that was where he had a much higher risk of being hurt.

Maybe Mr. Blake didn't like Jacques. Maybe when your name is Toe, you don't like anybody. Maybe one time Jacques gave Toe the finger. We'll never know unless we ask. But we didn't.

Then, in a game between the Montreal Canadiens and the New York Rangers, Plante was struck in the face by a shot from Andy Bathgate. Ouch. Plante decided to take a stand. He told his coach he wouldn't go back on the ice unless he was wearing his mask. The coach's only other option was to go in and play goal himself, and that wasn't gonna happen.

Plante won the standoff and went on to greatness as a goaltender, proving that the mask did not hurt his vision and allowed him to stop pucks with his head on purpose.

For a while, the rest of the hockey world ridiculed him for a lack of courage. At that time it was considered manly to stop 100-mile-an-hour shots with your face. But Plante stuck to his guns, and now goalies everywhere smile with real teeth and thank him for pioneering this safety feature.

✳ ✳ ✳

 I know I've mentioned this elsewhere in the book, but isn't it a sad comment on hockey in general and goalies in particular that it took them all that time to decide to protect their heads? There's a brain in there, right? Is that not worth protecting at least as much as your spleen?

Maybe it was some kind of macho thing to be a goalie and have the scars of five hundred slap shots on your face. That makes you a man. An ugly man, but still.

In Jacques's case, it seemed that management did not want him wearing the mask. I think it is always best for ownership if their players are great at playing the sport, but are otherwise complete idiots. It's much easier to fleece idiots. Makes you wonder if the introduction of the goalie mask, and helmets for the other players, correlates to the rise in power of the NHL Players' Association.

Whenever you bring a mask into a sport—or an event, or a court appearance—you're tapping into thirty-five thousand years of ritualistic history.

The mask has traditionally served many functions over the centuries. One of those was the disguising of identity. The NHL is aware of that one and has edited the rules of hockey to allow the ref to order a goalie to remove his mask so he can see who he is. But the larger and more meaningful reason for masks is that they were often used to represent the spirits of those who had gone before and to call on them to show up at whatever ritual—for example, a hockey game—was happening.

I would suggest that if a goalie mask was designed by a shaman or medicine man or voodoo aficionado, it could represent the spirits of former—and most likely, better—goalies. Some combination of Terry Sawchuk, Johnny Bower and Gump Worsley wouldn't hurt.

Another aspect of the historical mask is that it was used to indicate social status. You could present yourself as having success and power just by wearing a mask that showed images of those qualities.

Ancient Mask

A mask can also be used to improve your appearance. Everyone is intimidated by beauty, so having a mask that is better-looking than you are can only make you a more impressive goalie. It's kind of like the earliest form of Botox. So my advice is to forget the fancy masks offered by the latest flavour-of-the-month graphic artist and instead go with one of the ancient tribal masks.

Nobody's got the nerve to try to slip a puck through the five-hole of a twenty-five-thousand-year-old voodoo prince.

I'm not sure whether this is a physics or a geometry issue, but it seems to me that the introduction of the goalie mask creates an opportunity for the crafty goalie. Let's start with the dimensions of a standard NHL net.

It's gotta be four feet tall and six feet wide. That means the size of the opening is twenty-four square feet. I know the idea is that a really good goalie has the strength, hand-eye coordination

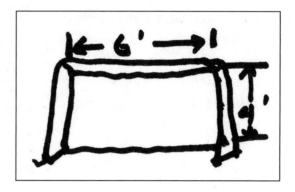

and reflexes to stop almost any puck that's shot at that twenty-four-square-foot hole. But doesn't it make sense to make that hole smaller if you can? Don't hurt yourself—the answer is yes. So let's

start with the size of the goalie himself. If he's two and a half feet wide and at least four feet tall, there's ten square feet of the twenty-four covered right there. But what if he was eight feet tall? Would that help?

The net is only four feet tall, so the extra height doesn't matter until he bends over. And even then, if he bends straight forward, he's still only taking up ten square feet of the opening. If I was an NHL coach, I would draft really, really tall goalies and then have them bend over sideways.

That would reduce the opening by another 3.75 square feet. Granted, the goalie's face would now be in the target zone, but the

human head is capable of swivelling, so that's a wash. And speaking of the human head, the goalie mask is, by definition, allowed to be bigger than the goalie's head, so in addition to the goalie being tall, you also want him to have a massive melon. You get a goalie with a head one and a half feet tall and one foot wide and then stick a mask on that thing and get him to drop his head down towards the ice, and you've reduced the twenty-four square feet of vulnerability down to six square feet.

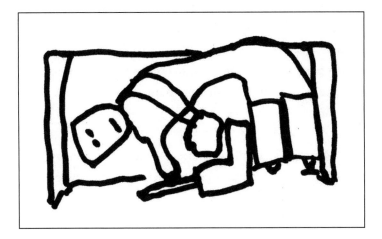

Get him a big glove and a goalie stick, and the shooter is left with about three square inches of net available, which is just slightly smaller than the puck. Looking at the picture above, I might add the suggestion of getting the goalie to switch the direction he's leaning every period, or possibly removing his spine completely, in order to avoid serious back problems.

And there's another scientific advantage that's available if you take the time and effort to figure it out. The puck moves over the ice and is guided by hockey sticks. That involves movement and friction. Any physicist will tell you that whenever you get those two elements happening together, you get a buildup of static electricity, and because of the surplus of electrons, that electricity always has a negative charge.

Now imagine that the goalie's uniform is made from a conductive fine metal mesh that is powered by a nine-volt battery in his goalie mask running a step-up transformer inside his jock. It may mean he'll never have children, but that's a small price to pay to win the Stanley Cup.

The plan works by creating a negatively charged field around the goalie, which rejects the similarly charged puck. He doesn't even have to make a save. He can just stand there and the puck will bounce off the invisible electronic shield.

I suppose the other team might come up with some clever way of making the puck positively charged, but I would consider that cheating.

To see how I used a goalie mask to assist with personal grooming, go to the Book of Inventions page at redgreen.com and click on "Mask."

GOWNLESS STRAP

René Beaulieu, Lodge Member and Fashion Guy

In the early '50s, Lodge member and avant-garde dress designer René Beaulieu shocked the world by creating a gownless evening strap. It never really caught on but was worn occasionally at nudist weddings.

Eventually, nudist weddings were discontinued for several reasons. There was nowhere to keep the ring, there were too many bouquet-tossing injuries and often the best man clearly wasn't.

René went on to invent toeless boots, pantless pockets and gloveless fingers before people decided he was just weird. René later admitted his actual name was Ron and went back to working at the library.

GREEN GARBAGE BAG
Henry Wasylyk

Harry Wasylyk, born on September 25, 1925, was a Canadian inventor from Winnipeg, Manitoba. He, along with partner Larry Hansen of Lindsay, Ontario, invented the green garbage bag in 1950. Try to imagine the excitement in the Wasylyk household that night.

Their first customer was the Winnipeg General Hospital. It wasn't until after Wasylyk and Hansen sold the invention to Larry's employer, the Union Carbide Company, that the green bags were marketed and sold for home use under the name Glad garbage bags.

They say the only things that are inevitable are death and taxes, but Henry knew garbage was pretty darn close.

I have no idea how much Hank and Larry got paid for the green garbage bag patent, but my guess is not nearly enough. I mean, talk about a product that exceeded expectations. I bet there's nowhere in the world that you could go and not see at least one green garbage bag by the side of the road. I wouldn't be surprised if there are some in outer space.

The boys probably just saw this as a cheap, sanitary, disposable garbage container, but it has turned into so much more. Green garbage bags are used as laundry hampers, suitcases, raincoats, groundsheets, roof patches, car windows, you name it. And what other product could simultaneously be a multipurpose, cost-effective, useful tool as well as the worst Halloween costume of all time?

If I was marooned on a desert island, I'd want to have a box of green garbage bags and a few rolls of duct tape. And a boat.

You budding inventors out there can learn a good lesson here. Way better to come up with a simple invention that everyone in the world has a need for rather than some complicated specific-use item that almost nobody cares about. Much smarter for Henry to invent a universal garbage bag than a better cesta for left-handed jai alai players. The simpler and more general you keep your invention, the less chance of it being a flash in the pan or a victim of a bad economy or a natural disaster.

As long as people are alive they will eat, sleep and create waste. There's a lot of competition in the eating and sleeping categories, but waste treatment is ripe for the picking. Sometimes you have to start at the bottom.

To see how we dealt with garbage at the Lodge, go to the Book of Inventions page at redgreen.com and click on "Garbage."

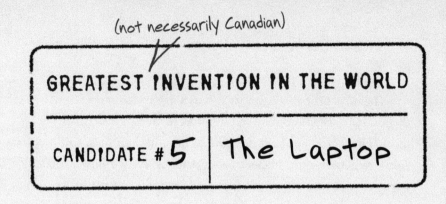

The laptop is a portable computer that folds up for carrying around and unfolds for use—kind of like a tent for nerds. But even for normal people who go on dates and don't have pocket protectors, this has become a pretty useful tool.

When they're in operation mode, laptops have a computer monitor built into their upper half, a keyboard built into their lower half, and, as many of you have discovered, a heat exhaust fan pointed directly at your shorts. Laptops can be run off a 110-volt AC plug, but since a portable computer needs to be portable, the main appeal of a laptop is the built-in battery that lets you use it in the car or on a plane or in a holding cell.

The battery life of a laptop varies, but a good rule of thumb is to first figure out how long it will take you to finish your current work project, and then subtract three minutes. That's when the battery will die. That is why the body of a laptop computer is built to withstand sudden impact with tile floors.

In the beginning, laptops were thought to be only going after a small number of people who might need a portable computer, like travelling salesmen or the military. Computer makers drastically underestimated the general public's desire to play spider solitaire or Minesweeper any time they damn well pleased.

Today, the laptop computer has been replaced by the tablet. That's because after twenty years of playing video games, people have put on so much weight they no longer have laps.

RATING: I know you're shocked, but the laptop ain't it either. Candidate #6 is on deck.

HARD CUP JOCKSTRAP
Jack Cartledge

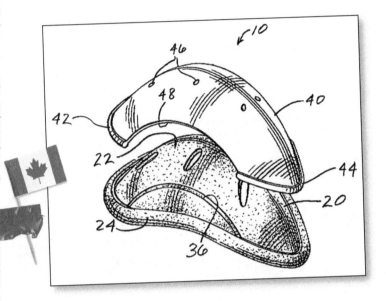

n 1927, Jack Cartledge (what's in a name?) of the Guelph Elastic Hosiery Company patented his idea for an upgraded jockstrap. His brainchild included a hard cup for extra protection. The reasons for this upgrade were not recorded, but anyone who's ever had a bicycle chain break while they were riding uphill was extremely grateful.

On the other hand, anybody who's watched the amount of scratching that goes on in the dugout during a major-league baseball game might not be so enthusiastic.

✳ ✳ ✳

This is one of those inventions that seems pretty logical and straightforward—but don't be fooled. This baby is a combination of designs that have been percolating for hundreds of years.

First of all, even in 1927, the idea of protecting body parts with hard shields was not a new concept. The armour worn by medieval knights was basically a jock for the whole body. But over the years, as society became more civilized and warfare became less personal, the need for armour on a day-to-day basis pretty much disappeared. It only remained necessary for the police or the military or anyone playing contact sports.

Now, it says in his bio that Mr. Cartledge, who came up with the hard cup breakthrough, played rugby, one of the roughest sports known to man. These guys don't wear shoulder pads or knee pads or anything. My guess is that from 1927 on, the only protection they wore was the hard cup jockstrap.

Why would they only need to protect that area? What kind of an opponent would choose the genitalia as their prime target? They would have to either be heathens or very short—or, worst of all, very short heathens. I think there's a whole other reason, but before I get to that, let's look at more evidence.

I'm referring, of course, to the game of hockey. Hockey players adopted the hard cup jockstrap as soon as it came out in the late 1920s. But it wasn't until 1979, fifty years later, that helmets became mandatory. So for fifty years the same guys who wore a hard cup jockstrap every game would never even *think* of wearing a helmet. What does that say about their priorities?

That's the reason I was referring to earlier. Historically, men put different values on different body parts, and the genital area is always high in the pecking order. And it's not just because it's a more reliable source of entertainment than many of the others.

The muscles and bones and organs of the body are the "here and now" of human existence; the genitals are the future. If your father or grandfather played sports, you may owe your very existence to Jack Cartledge.

But there's a downside to all of this. As useful and helpful as the hard cup jockstrap became, it placed a burden on Jack's own descendants. Of course, I'm taking about the burden of embarrassment. Imagine meeting someone in Guelph and going to their home, which turns out to be a mansion. Then the painful conversation begins.

"What a beautiful home."

"Thanks. It belonged to my grandfather."

"Really? He must have been very successful."

"Yes . . . yes, he was."

"What did he do?"

"Ah . . . He was involved with sports."

"He was a professional athlete?"

"Nope . . . Wow, look at those clouds."

"So did your grandfather own a team or a league or something?"

"No, he was just really an insider in the sports industry."

"So he was an athletic supporter."

"You could say that."

I also think there's more value to the hard cup than first meets the eye. It's compact, strong, aerodynamic and even artistic. I'm surprised that design was never embraced by the automotive industry.

Someone once told me that a man looks at his car as an extension of, or even replacement for, his own manhood. That is not the kind of thing you like to hear when you drive a Possum Van, but I was thinking: What might a car look like if was designed as a protector of, rather than replacement for, said manhood?

The 1932 Porsche Joxster*

Imagine the look on your teammates' faces when you pull up to the arena driving a brand new Porsche Joxster sports coupe (pronounced "cup"). Smooth and sleek, with a hard finish that will protect your loved ones from whatever life throws at you. Seats two in the front and one in the back. An all-natural instrument cluster, and wait'll you see the horn! Powered by a two-cylinder, four-stroke engine and stick shift, the Jockster is a big hit with the ladies. (Elasticized cotton garage available as an option.) Drop by your local dealership and take one for a test drive. The Porsche Joxster: Feel the Itch.

Available in hardtop only.

HAWAIIAN PIZZA
Sam Panopoulos

According to what I've been told, Hawaiian pizza was invented in 1962 by Sam Panopoulos of Chatham, Ontario. At the time, he was co-owner of a place called the Satellite Restaurant.

So what I'm saying is, a man of Greek descent added a fruit from Hawaii to a dish from Italy, and he did it in the country of Canada in a restaurant from outer space. His creation has had mixed reviews ever since. In Australia, Hawaiian pizza is the most popular kind. In Iceland, they say it should be against the law. Most people fall somewhere in between. But however you feel about it, it was something new and it belongs to us.

There are a lot of great things about pizza. It's fast, it's easy, it's delivered. If you have a phone, you can make a pizza. And you have almost unlimited choices as to what you want on it. You can have all the food groups lying there if that makes you happy. But remember, salt is not a food group.

You can even have half of your pizza topped one way and the other half topped another, which has saved more than one marriage. And as all college kids know, pizza leaves no dishes or cutlery to be washed up.

All that choice can create serious problems for customers. If you've ever had four people try to agree on what kind of pizza to order, you know what I mean. Let's start with the toppings. You have about fifty to choose from, but the weekly special is always an extra large with three toppings for $9.95. You and your friends will starve to death waiting for everyone to agree on those three toppings. That's because they're not normal, go-along-to-get-along toppings. They all have attitude—anchovies and hot peppers and spicy sausage and onions and bacon. All strong flavours and, other than the cheese, there's nothing that everybody likes.

Moose Thompson always started the process by ordering a plain cheese pizza so he'd have something to munch on while deciding what the real pizza order is going to be. Helped make him the man he is today.

But then, even if everybody compromises and agrees on three toppings that they sort of like, now you gotta pick the crust—thin crust, thick crust, deep dish, cheese-stuffed. And what about whole wheat or gluten-free or dairy-free or no sauce or overdone or underdone? It's easier to buy a birthday gift for Sybil than it is to order a one-size-fits-all pizza.

It's a brilliant marketing plan. You don't order a pizza, you order two or three or four. Instead of having a pizza that nobody really likes, you end up with four boxes of leftovers that nobody can agree on.

That's just the way it is when you try to make everybody happy. I blame democracy.

ICE HOCKEY
Canada?

"YE GUDE OLDE DAYS."

The game of ice hockey was more or less the winter version of field hockey, which had been played in Europe for centuries before Canada was even thought of. But in Canada, fields are only usable for about three weeks a year. So instead, different versions of ice hockey popped up from coast to coast as the field hockey game was changed to fit the colder climate.

That all led to the first official indoor game of ice hockey, held in Montreal on March 3, 1875. The game featured nine players a side and used a wooden puck. The word *puck* comes from the old Gaelic word *puc*, which meant to poke or punch. Eventually the players' fists were used for that purpose, and the game we know was born.

✳ ✳ ✳

 If you look around the world, you'll notice that different countries have different national sports, and most of the time those sports are suited to the geography and climate of the country and to the temperament of its citizens. Spain has bullfighting, Italy has soccer, Russia has chess. And of course, Canada has hockey. America also has hockey, but it's mostly Canadians playing it.

Hockey is perfectly suited for Canada.

- You play it in the winter, which in Canada is most of the time.
- You only need six guys on each team. If it needed more than that, there wouldn't be any Canadians left to watch.
- You get to use a stick. Canadians don't carry guns.
- Pucks are cheap. So are many Canadians.
- You get to wear a lot of clothes. Really long wool socks and big loose sweaters. Canadians like to be warm and casual.
- Hockey is passive-aggressive. You can pretend to be going for the puck as you knock a guy into the penalty box. A lot of Canadians are passive-aggressive. Some are aggressive-aggressive. Others are passive-passive.
- You get to embarrass people. When you get a penalty in football, you disappear to the bench for a while. When you get a penalty in hockey, you have to sit in the penalty box on full display for two minutes or more. Oh, the shame. Canadians love that.

Norb "No Nonsense" Cochrane,
Rink Rat and Local Gamer

- The trophy is huge. The Stanley Cup is one of the largest trophies in any sport, towering over legendary greats like Gump Worsley.
- Hockey gave us *Hockey Night in Canada*, the most popular television show in the history of Canada. *Euchre Night in Canada* would have been a disaster.

Norb Cochrane was looking to create a spinoff sport with the same tremendous popularity of hockey.

He had played hockey as a young man, building a reputation as an enforcer. He would often get into a fight with the other team's star player. Usually during the first period, but sometimes he would go into the dressing room before the game and slap the guy upside the head with a wet towel. On occasion he would cold-cock players at random as they were coming off the team bus.

He wasn't much of a hockey player, but he excelled at broomball, thanks largely to his family's extensive janitorial background. Here again, his aggressive nature got in the way. He started a fight during the final playoff broomball game. It was a best-of-seven series and Norb's team was already up three games to none and looking to sweep. Before the opening whistle, somebody on the other team made a derogatory remark about the small size of Norb's broom, and he went off the handle. He punched out every player, both coaches, and a hot dog vendor before he was finally whisked out of the building. Faced with the overwhelming challenge of creating a new game and making himself look smart,

Norb focused all of his attention, other than during bar hours, on finding a form of hockey that would be new and exciting and would make him rich and better-looking.

Norb thought that if he was famous, he could punch people and they would thank him. Five years later, he came up with the concept that would make him what he is today—unemployed. Instead of ice hockey, Norb created snow hockey. A game very similar to ice hockey but a bit slower and easier.

The game, as you may have already guessed, was played on snow, and instead of hockey sticks, the players used snow shovels—called "snovels" for short and also because Norb couldn't spell "snow shovel."

The forwards and defencemen had regular coal shovel–style snovels, but the goalie had the wider plow-style snovel. In keeping with the theme, the puck was a snowball, called the "snowball." The rest of the game was very similar to hockey.

Norb's lawyer warned him that he could not call the game "hockey" without creating a lot of problems. Norb considered punching out every player and manager and team owner in the NHL, but when he thought about what that would require in terms of effort and expense and lonely nights on the road, he reconsidered.

It made sense to Norb that because ice hockey is called "hockey," snow hockey should be called "snockey." Similarly, "He shoots, he scores!" became "He snoots, we snore!" The goal was to get a goal. To get the snowball past the goalie into the net using a normal-speed "wrist snot" or the dreaded, lightning-fast "slap snot." Because the game was played on snow, there were no lines and therefore no offside.

Scoring was usually high, often hitting three digits for the winning team. One of the many problems with the game was that fans could easily make a snowball and throw it at the goalie. Or the ref. Or the visiting team. Or each other. Luckily, there were no fans, so Norb dodged a bullet on that one.

A more important issue was the snowball's habit of increasing in size as it rolled during the game. One playoff game was tied at 112 and had to be called after thirty-seven overtime periods because the snowball had grown larger than either of the nets. When the concept was on its last snowy legs, Norb got an offer from the owners of the Possum Lake Threshers, a farm team for Massey Ferguson, to have demonstration snockey games on Possum Lake before each Thresher game.

It would be good publicity for the new game and a cheap way for the Threshers to get the ice cleared off. Norb thanked them for their offer and then punched each one in the face, permanently ending negotiations.

To see Bill play hockey, go to the Book of Inventions page at redgreen.com and click on "Hockey."

IMAX
William Shaw

William Shaw, born in 1939 and a longtime resident of Streetsville, Ontario, became the inventor of the IMAX film format in 1968, along with the other members of the IMAX Corporation. They had been hired to run a multiscreen movie at Expo 67 by trying to use a bunch of projectors to supply different parts of the picture. It was tough to do and never really worked all that well, so the group decided to try to develop one projector and film type that could fill a large screen all on its own. William was hired as the technical guy and was the main force behind the whole shebang. Like the projector itself, Bill was bright and focused.

After his death in 2002, one of his IMAX partners, Graeme Ferguson, said, "If it hadn't been for Bill, there would be no IMAX."

✳ ✳ ✳

I'm not sure exactly when this happened, but at some point in history, bigger became better. It didn't use to be that way. The Alamo or the pyramids or the *Mona Lisa* or even the Statue of Liberty are pretty small when compared to Trump Tower or the Dallas Cowboys' stadium. The Old Masters were going for perfection, which, although impossible, is less impossible on a small project.

And everything was smaller back then—houses, budgets, people. Being small was a sign of humility, which at that time was seen as a good thing. And this is just my opinion, but I think that age of artistic modesty began during the Renaissance and ended when Jerry Lee Lewis released "Whole Lotta Shakin' Goin' On." I don't remember the year, but I was in Grade 8 for the first time, so it had to be the '50s. That was the end of the shrinking violet. It was the end of the shrinking everything—egos, fortunes, hairstyles and hamburgers. And people.

Since then, the size of the average guy in North America has gone up 30 per cent in height and weight. Well, okay, 2 per cent in height and 28 per cent in weight. And since most of us are getting bigger, we'd rather think that bigger is better. IMAX fit right in with that line of reasoning. And it's probably going to keep goin' that way. Maybe one day they'll be able to project the image of a sunny day in the sky above St. John's.

IMAX is a theatrical experience that really suits the Canadian culture and lifestyle. We're used to wide-open spaces, we like everybody to be able to see what's going on and we have a history of always looking at the big picture. The self-effacing, modest nature of Canadians makes us hesitant to sit in the front row, and with IMAX, you don't have to. IMAX has even affected Hollywood. Many big-budget movies are released in IMAX and sometimes IMAX 3D. IMAX is also the reason most modern movie actors trim their nose hairs.

The owners of our local movie house, Robert Johnson and his partner, John Robertson (he's the one with the bigger thing between his legs), were fascinated by the IMAX concept and were interested in bringing the technology to their theatre. Unfortunately, they were missing all of the key elements required to install the equipment.

They found it difficult to get financing from anyone who knew them or asked to look at their books. And with only a sixty-amp service, the theatre did not have enough power to run an IMAX projector *and* make popcorn. It also didn't help that their cinema was in the basement of the Presbyterian church.

They thought about declaring bankruptcy, but they had done that so many times before. They wanted to try something new. So instead, they took the IMAX approach but applied it to other senses.

The Possum Lake Drive-In Theatre had recently gone under, and Johnson and Robertson were able to pick up all of the drive-in speakers by simply hooking them onto their car windows and driving away. They attached all 239 speakers to the inside walls of the theatre and then con-nected them to the projector ampli-fier. They removed the curtains and carpeting and any other soft, sound-absorbing material from the cinema. They then turned the amplifier up full, and Earmax was born.

John Robertson and Robert Johnson, Owners of Possum Lake Cinema and Chair Storage

The first movie presented in Earmax was *Gone with the Wind*, which, according to ticket sales, turned out to be prophetic. There were a few problems. The sound level inside the theatre was incredibly loud. It hovered around 150 decibels, which made it impossible to hold a soft drink.

Instead of going to the movie, people would just go into the church upstairs with a lunchbox. Sitting in the pews, they could hear the movie well enough to pick up the storyline. It was the first time anyone had ever skipped a movie to go to church.

Another drawback for Robert and John was that they couldn't afford first-run movies, so everyone had already seen whatever they were showing. People were calling in with numerous noise complaints, but the boys were unaware because when the movie was playing, they couldn't hear the phone ring.

After two weeks of disappointing results, they shut down Earmax. That was the beginning of the end for Robert and John. For a while, they toyed with the concept of Nosemax, but the cost of scented aerosol spray cans was a big hurdle. Locals say they did manage to pull off a one-night showing of *Animal Farm*, and they still haven't been able to get the smell out.

They eventually closed the theatre and went back to doing what they were best at, which was nothing.

To see my attempt at making a portable big screen, go to the Book of Inventions page at redgreen.com and click on "Screen."

INSTANT FOOD
Edward Asselbergs

Edward Asselbergs invented a way to preserve food by first boiling and then quick-freezing it. Just add water to the resulting dry powder, and you're back in business. The process worked on many different kinds of food. He used the technique to create instant fish, cheese and meat. He also made instant mashed potatoes, and that process is still in use today.

At first, his instant fish, cheese and meat were not received well by the public (no kidding), but when he switched to instant mashed potatoes, things went a lot better. Attaboy, Eddie.

✳ ✳ ✳

This is one of those examples of how a great scientist and brilliant inventor can be really, really stupid. Okay, his process of dehydration was real smart, nobody denies that. But why start with meat? Or fish? What are the chances somebody wants to make a hamburger by adding a cup of water to a hockey puck?

How do you expect people to react to dehydrated pickerel? "It tastes like a fish out of water to me."

Or dehydrated cheese? Really, Mr. Asselbergs? You should have just started with mashed potatoes. They're mostly water anyway. When you add the water back in, you're replacing the biggest part. Of course it works. And the consistency is okay too. Adding water to dried potato crystals to make mashed potatoes feels almost natural. We add water to flour to make paste, so it's not that much of a stretch, in either the look or the texture or the taste.

But I wonder if Mr. Asselbergs realized the powerful impact his instant mashed potatoes were going to have on society. Next thing you know, we have instant coffee, instant powdered milk, instant rice, instant credit, instant replay and the ultimate, instant gratification. It was a game changer. It marked the end of patience. If I can make mashed potatoes in forty-five seconds, why does it take two months to get a doctor's appointment?

In a lot of ways, it defined our modern society. We all read about the Renaissance and the Industrial Age, and now we will go down in history as the generation that didn't have time to make mashed potatoes.

Over the history of the English language, certain words have either had their meanings changed or diminished or obliterated all together. *Instant* is one of those words. So are *awesome*, *warranty* and *fiancé*.

By definition, *instant* means "immediate," "simultaneous," "at exactly the same moment." It doesn't mean "soon" or "in five minutes" or "quick enough." When something is instantaneous, like a nuclear explosion, it happens pretty fast. There's not a lot of lag time between detonation and *kaboom*. That's what instant is supposed to be. If instant pudding were true to its name, you'd just snap your fingers and *poof*, there's a chocolate blob in your favourite bowl.

So when they call this invention "instant food," they don't really mean it. What they're saying is that this method of making something is so much faster than any of the alternatives that it's close to being instantaneous, even though it doesn't quite get there.

And from a marketing perspective, it would be tough to sell something called "doesn't take very long compared to what you're used to pudding." So sure, using the word *instant* is a bit of a white lie, but without those there'd be almost no human communication.

Howard Boschler lived in the Possum Lake area, where for several years he had been able to survive without the benefit of gainful employment. He did it by having a keen sense of what people would buy and then selling it to them. He watched quietly while the instant food phenomenon gained traction.

On his sixtieth birthday, his friends both pitched in and bought him a small jar of sea monkeys, which made Howard realize that the "instant" approach was not restricted to food. The next spring, he went door to door selling "instant smarts." It was a coarse powder to which you add water and drink, and presto, you were smarter. "Instant smarts" was an instant hit. The next day, one of Possum Lake's resident intellectuals (they stand out) recognized the powder as regular table salt.

When confronted, Howard replied by asking, "Well, would you buy powder from me again?" The answer was, of course, no, to which Howard said, "Well then, you're smarter. You're welcome."

Howard Boschler, Local Opportunist

INSTANT REPLAY
George Retzlaff

George Retzlaff, a producer for the CBC on the very popular *Hockey Night in Canada*, was the first to come up with a wet-film replay of a hockey goal during the 1955–56 season.

The replay took about thirty seconds to be ready to show, and was the first of its kind. George got into trouble, though, as he did not warn the ad agency (MacLaren) in advance that he was planning to use the new technique, so they missed the chance to market it. Wow.

Also, the sister production studio in Montreal did not have the same equipment, and so George had broken the in-house CBC rule that production in both studios had to be on the same level. Double wow.

He did not use the method again. Can you blame him? The same brain trust that said no to George's ingenuity said yes to my television show. Not sure how I feel about that now.

✳ ✳ ✳

What a great message to send out to future Canadian innovators: Don't do anything until we find a way to make money at it, and you're not allowed to chew gum unless you brought enough for everyone. Let's just be glad George didn't find a cure for cancer. The drug companies would have been ticked and the health care bosses wouldn't let him use it until every hospital had one.

And what a message to send to George. "I know you've just invented something that will be a boon to our industry in terms of audience appreciation and revenue generated, but it will also create a lot of political problems with our advertisers and sister stations, and that's not what you're here for, George. Now, just sit there and push those buttons like you were hired to do. I'll do the thinking, thank you very much. *Merci beaucoup.*"

Sometimes I think any form of progress is a miracle.

The rest of the television world took the idea and ran with it. It became an immediate staple of every televised sport. It was kind of like instant home movies. We'd all seen home movies before, but that ten-day delay while the guy at the drugstore developed them was enough to remove any desire to watch them.

The ability to see something and then to be able to immediately watch it again, while you were still sort of interested, was pretty sweet. But what happened after that is the interesting part.

The ability to look at things the way they were in the past had been around since the cavemen drew picutres of fires on their walls. Artists got better, and then we got still cameras and then we got movie cameras and then we got instant still cameras and then we got George, whose idea was really the first instant movie camera.

But it was all passive observation. You could look at what happened in the past, but you couldn't in any way alter its outcome. Kind of like going back in a time machine but not being allowed to change anything.

But then one day, all that went out the window. It was probably the fans who made it happen. In the old days, when a ref made a bad call, the fans would get mad for an instant, throw out a couple of boos and then suck it up and get back to the action. With George's instant replay, the fans could watch the bad call over and over and over and over again. And so could the team owners. And the refs. And the wives of the refs. Something had to give.

The refs had always been suspected of being the bad guys, but now there was proof. So one by one the sports started changing rules, using the instant replay as an opportunity for the refs to make sure they'd got it right and change their rulings if they hadn't. And then they allowed the coaches to challenge many of the rulings during the game.

The weirdest example has to be tennis. In other sports, the instant replay involves showing the taped footage from multiple angles at slow speeds in order to get the call right. Not so in tennis. In tennis, when a player challenges a call, the instant replay is a cartoon. It's a digital picture of a tennis ball landing on a digital court. Huh? I know you are wondering about the shot that was just made, Mr. Federer, but watch this mini-movie of a digital ball landing out, does that help? No, it doesn't.

But thankfully, the other sports have the sense to show a *real* replay when called for. Now we got a true time machine. You can go back into the past and fix what was wrong. And all thanks to George. Thank you, George. I hope the CBC threw you a huge retirement party, and I hope you got a better watch than the guy in Montreal.

———

I wish instant replay worked in the real world. It would be good if you could go back and change the things you did wrong. It's really the only reason to have instant replay. Often when we're coming home from a party, my wife will give me an instant replay of the entire evening and it really isn't helpful to either one of us.

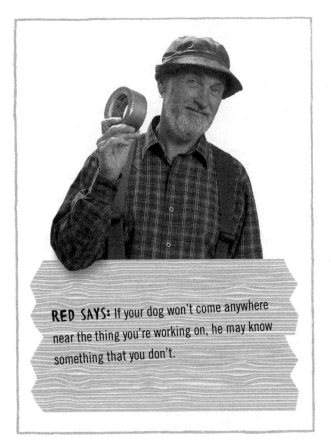

RED SAYS: If your dog won't come anywhere near the thing you're working on, he may know something that you don't.

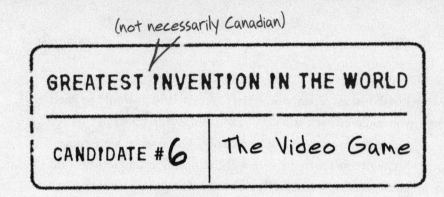

(not necessarily Canadian)

GREATEST INVENTION IN THE WORLD

CANDIDATE #6 | The Video Game

Video games have been around for about fifty years now, and to be honest I still don't see the appeal. I'm sure you're surprised by that. You would think being in a world where you can do anything you want and experience no real-life consequences would be appealing to a guy with as many injuries as I've had, but no. I guess I just prefer the real thing.

These games are in this new world they call "virtual reality." Who wants *virtual* reality when we have actual reality? I don't. But some do. Ever since Pong came out in the '70s, video games have been a serious time waster. Sure, over the years the graphics have gotten better and the storylines more complicated. Some game manufacturers have enough money now that they can hire Hollywood actors to voice the in-game characters, giving fans a sense that maybe this was money well spent.

This industry has really taken off with younger people. Seems kind of sad to me that the next generation prefers an imaginary world to the real thing. I hope that's not my fault.

And now, for a fee, you can go online and watch someone else play a video game. Live. Think about that. The guy playing the game has checked out of the actual world, which is bad enough, but the guy watching is even one step farther away than that. He doesn't even have the confidence to step into an *imaginary* world.

Good luck with the real one.

RATING: You lose, please play again. Maybe Candidate #7.

INSULIN
Frederick Banting

Frederick Banting was born in Alliston, Ontario, on November 14, 1891. After flunking out of a general arts program at U of T, he petitioned to join the medical program, was accepted and began classes in 1913. Good to know that if you're not good enough in school to get a B.A. in fly fishing, you can always be a doctor.

After the war broke out, his medical class was fast-tracked, so he graduated in December 1916 and went right into the army. Merry Christmas. He received a medal for heroism for continuing to aid other soldiers after being injured himself, which marked the first but not last time he would save lives.

While getting ready to deliver a lecture in 1920, he read the work of a few other scientists on the role of the pancreas and was anxious to begin his own testing on the subject. He approached J.J.R. Macleod at U of T, who reluctantly gave Banting some research space and the use of an assistant named Charles Best while Macleod was away for the summer.

Banting and Best's research lead to the invention of insulin, and eventually its first use on human patients.

Banting and Macleod received the Nobel Prize in 1923 for the invention of insulin, but Banting was cheesed off that Macleod had received the award with him instead of Best. Banting decided to share his portion of the award money with Best. He didn't want to see Best bested because he knew Best was best.

✳ ✳ ✳

 Insulin is a great, great discovery. Thousands, maybe even millions of lives have been saved or at least extended by it. So what is it about humans that they take a miracle like insulin and immediately start imagining how similar medical breakthroughs must be right around the corner?

I say "humans," but really what I'm talking about is "fat guys." If science can find a way to allow a diabetic to eat candy and live, surely it can find a way for a glutton to eat twelve cheeseburgers and still stay slim. And the added misconception, which makes it doubly dangerous, is that the patient doesn't have to make any adjustments at all. The belief is that the diabetic doesn't have to alter his diet, or exercise regimen, because the insulin will take care of everything. Surely there's a pill or injection coming that will juice up your metabolism or turbocharge your large intestine so that all those calories you take in won't be hanging around long enough to do any damage.

Of course, now we're tapping into a behavioural pattern that's at the core of all human existence: self-delusion. "I'm fine. I'm sure I'm fine. I'm not perfect, but nobody is. There are people who are better than me, but there are also people who are worse than me. I'm good. Despite what my boss and my doctor and my wife and my mirror and my urine tests say, I'm fine."

I know that advertisers and movie producers and the Fox News Channel believe that we all like to see young, good-looking, fit people. And we do. But not totally and not all the time. Once in a while we need to see a fat, ugly, disgusting guy. Somebody worse than us. When we look at the attractive people, we think, "Wow, I wish I looked like that." But we know we can't. Whereas when we look at Bluto, we think, "Wow, at least I don't look like that."

If you know you can't be the best, you pride yourself on not being the worst. It's a lot easier to be a fat guy than to be the fattest guy. Doctors are partially to blame because they lie. They tell the patient that he's gotta lose a hundred pounds or he'll be dead in two years. Then, on the second day of the diet, the patient meets a guy who's a hundred pounds heavier than him and five years older. He thinks, "Wait a minute, *he* didn't die. I probably won't either . . . Oh look, a Dairy Queen."

Really fat guys are like the canary in the coal mines for moderately fat guys. They're the test pilots for obesity. They get sent out to see if the ice is thick enough for the snowmobiles, if an all-bacon diet really will kill you, and just how low are the standards of the girls in this bar.

I think if you're a doctor or a medical scientist, you gotta be very careful. If you ever come up with a drug that guarantees health and happiness, people will just take that and go back to the couch. If that happens, humanity will be lost, nothing will ever be accomplished and, more important, this will be the last book about inventions ever written. Nobody wants that.

In 1974, local bar entertainer Burt Franklin, inspired by the creation of insulin and its effects on helping the pancreas do its job, decided to try something similar for his ailing liver. Burt was the resident magician at Duffy's Tavern in downtown Possum Lake. He would entertain the clientele by performing card tricks and pulling coins out of various body orifices, sometimes his own.

The reviews were mixed. As were Burt's beverages. That's because the bar paid Burt in drinks and he always cashed those cheques before leaving the building. As a result, Burt's liver was in rough shape. He had a hard time getting life insurance, and the local fire department had declared that Burt was not, under any circumstances, to be cremated.

Burt Franklin, Local Entertainer

One night after Burt had been significantly overpaid at the pub, he caught a PBS special on insulin and decided to start concocting his own medical breakthrough. He named it "cod liver ale." It was a mix of alcoholic beverages, Advil, a mild laxative, toothpaste, windshield washer/antifreeze, four jujubes, a pomegranate and gum from under the bar.

Burt tried the formula every morning for a week. He didn't notice any change in his health, other than one day he burped on the bus and set off the smoke alarm. By the second week, Burt saw his doctor, who performed an MRI only to discover that Burt's liver was now the size of an adult raccoon.

The doctor ordered Burt to stop taking the homemade medicine and quit his gig at Duffy's. He then arranged for Burt to entertain patients in the hospital waiting room, where he would be paid in organs. Over the next three months Burt received four kidneys, two spleens and a Wurlitzer before he got the liver he so desperately needed.

JOLLY JUMPER
Olivia Poole

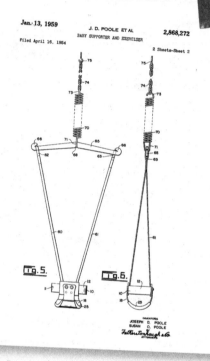

Jan. 13, 1959
J. D. POOLE ET AL
2,868,272
BABY SUPPORTER AND EXERCISER
Filed April 16. 1954
2 Sheets-Sheet 2

INVENTORS
JOSEPH D. POOLE
SUSAN O. POOLE
Fetherstonhaugh & Co.
ATTORNEYS

Patent Drawing for the Jolly Jumper

Olivia Poole came up with the first Jolly Jumper in Toronto in 1910. She got the idea from her Aboriginal heritage: the papooses that First Nations people used to carry their babies around. Pretty similar to what most parents do today. It keeps the baby safe and keeps your hands free and is a great back warmer. The Jolly Jumper could just as easily have been called the Bouncing Papoose.

Olivia had the first one made for her own baby out of a cloth diaper, a steel spring and an axe handle. If you did that today, you'd be getting a visit from the Children's Aid Society.

Olivia and her son brought the product to market in 1948, and received the patent in 1957. By then, her son was almost fifty and was probably getting a little tired of demonstrating the darn thing.

 This is one of those inventions that make me nostalgic for the times when you always had a little danger mixed in with the fun. We never wore bicycle helmets. We played lawn darts. We ate peanut butter. And we had Jolly Jumpers.

They hooked onto the door trim over the kid's head. Mind you, that was when door trim was made of wood, not polypropylene. And even if the thing did fall down, kids were allowed to sustain minor injuries back then. It was even encouraged. Helped prepare us for a world where sometimes things don't go your way.

Kids aren't allowed to think that way anymore. Maybe it's better now, I don't know. But I don't regret having a BB gun or tobogganing in a cardboard box or perfecting the Jolly Jumper spin move that allowed me to see into two different rooms at the same time. It was better than the TV, which only had one channel.

In 1958, local hardware store owner George Roloff was looking for help dealing with Heinrik, his very rambunctious one-year-old. George searched the shelves of his store, silently wishing he'd bought a pharmacy, when he spotted the Jolly Jumper.

George Roloff

George recognized the potential, but also knew his son would soon tire of jumping up and down in one spot. He went over to the household section and picked up a hundred feet of clothesline and a half-dozen pulleys. He then went home and mounted the clothesline and pulleys to hang horizontally from the ceiling, not unlike streetcar cables, creating a small indoor track.

He hung the Jolly Jumper from a really strong clothes peg, and Heinrik was able to jump all around the house without bumping into walls or ornaments. When George's wife came home, he was drinking beer on the porch.

She was about to ask where Heinrik was when she saw him bounce by the living room window. She didn't take it well. George tried to explain the brilliance of the clothesline amusement ride, but in the end, she hung him out to dry.

Local adventurer Eunice Fairchild saw a lot more potential in the Jolly Jumper than just a way to keep small children occupied— something that did not concern her anyway, as she did not have children and indeed had never been married. Or had a boyfriend. Or been on a date.

Her first step was to increase the size and strength of the harness and elasticized straps. She used the bodice from a parachute that had been handed to her as she was pushed out of a plane while vacationing.

She also had a supply of truck inner tubes that she was planning to use to make figure-enhancing casual wear, but decided instead to cut the rubber into long strips and tie them together to give her the combination of strength and stretchiness that a lot of women go for.

Another drawback that Eunice noticed about the Jolly Jumper was that you were stuck in one place. She decided not only to create an adult-sized jumper, but to add technology that would allow it to be an effective means of transportation that appealed to people who were either on a tight budget or who were working to cut down on their carbon footprint.

Eunice Fairchild,
Experimental Person

One day as Ms. Fairchild was riding through town on her Schwinn, wondering why the world was so weird and not really paying attention to where she was going, she ran into a window washer's stepladder. She met the window washer a few seconds later.

She meant to apologize, but when she saw the stepladder tangled up with her bike, she knew it was the breakthrough she was looking for. She rushed home and worked all night putting it together. After sleeping most of the next two days, she awoke, took the thing apart and put it back together properly.

The Happy Hopper was born.

The rider starts by jumping up and down, but that is only to build momentum. After a few jumps, the rider springs forward, causing him or her to rise into the air as the unit moves forward. Repeating the leaping motion builds up speed and allows the Happy Hopper to cover significant distances with each stride.

Eunice's first trip on the machine was to go down to the patent office to register her ingenious device. When she arrived, she was unable to stop. She was forced out of town by her own momentum. She was never seen again in Possum Lake, but someone said she got a job in Port Asbestos as a bouncer.

Several others struggled to find a use for the device. Local road maintenance workers tried using it to paint dotted lines on the highway. The high school gym teacher used it to train hurdlers. Possum Lake's resident daredevil, Rutger Lapsich, put on a display where he got into the machine and ran barefoot across a freshly fertilized cornfield.

About halfway across, Rutger had a little too much leg kick, which caused him to flip over and complete the run upside down. He was relatively unhurt, but he retired the Happy Hopper. And his hair smelled funny for the rest of his life.

KEROSENE
Abraham Gesner

Abraham Gesner was born in Nova Scotia's Annapolis Valley in the early 1800s. In his late teens he joined the merchant marine, but after experiencing the excitement of a couple of shipwrecks, he packed it in and became a doctor, which is likely the first and last time that particular career path has been taken. But you know that old expression about how you can take the man out of the adventure, but you can't take the adventure out of the man? Neither do I, but it's true.

So in between patients, Abe studied geology, and in 1836 he discovered big deposits of iron ore and coal in Nova Scotia. He went on to make geological discoveries in New Brunswick and Quebec, and his medical patients started having a tough time getting an appointment. However, Abraham got one—he was named provincial geologist for New Brunswick in 1838.

But his big breakthrough was when he created a process to refine a liquid fuel from coal bitumen and oil shale. He called the stuff "kerosene." It burned cleaner and was cheaper than anything else on the market. Pretty soon it was powering street lamps in Halifax and eventually all over North America.

Abraham's only obstacle was finding a way to make more kerosene and make it faster and cheaper. Then along came petroleum, which is a way easier starting point for kerosene, and that did the trick.

In 1933, Imperial Oil put up a memorial in Camp Hill Cemetery in Halifax as a tribute to Abraham and all of his contributions.

✳ ✳ ✳

 I could have written a lot more about Abraham Gesner, but I didn't because it was starting to make me feel like a useless dork. The guy did good. We can all see that.

So I'd like to focus on what I would call a side effect of his invention that is maybe as important as the invention itself. Yes, he invented kerosene, which was used all around the world, but what they didn't mention was that Abe was simultaneously inventing camping.

Up until kerosene same along, camping wasn't camping. It was living in the woods. No light, no heat, no cooking. Kerosene changed all that. Now you could have a kerosene lamp to light the way so you didn't have to go to the bathroom right beside the tent. And a kerosene stove to cook whatever you caught or brought—or not. And just raw kerosene to give that old campfire a kick-start.

So we all owe a lot to Mr. Gesner and his work. Especially me. When they first got married, my parents went camping a lot. If it wasn't for kerosene, I might not even be here.

LACROSSE
William George Beers

L acrosse started way back when with the Aboriginal game of *baggataway*, which despite being fun to say was a pretty violent activity. It had hundreds or even thousands of players playing at one time. And no ref.

It was a game used to train young warriors for war, as well as to settle tribal disputes. It would have been used to keep the young people off the streets if there were any streets. In 1844, the Montreal Olympic Club organized a team to play against the Native people. In 1856, the Montreal Lacrosse Club was founded, and the first written rules were developed. White men love rules. Over the next ten years, Montreal Lacrosse Club member and dentist William George Beers kept tweaking the game until it turned into the sport it is today.

William George Beers, the Father of Professional Lacrosse

✻ ✻ ✻

Sounds to me like the early days of lacrosse were closer to war than sport. Maybe the true beginning dates back to the caveman using a tree branch as a club. It was a big deal for man to make tools, because it proved he had enough smarts to figure that he could hit something harder with a stick than he could with his hand. (And that it wouldn't hurt.) Not just because of the increase in mass, but more importantly, the increase in velocity that happens when the arm length is stretched by three or four feet. It's why the Tyrannosaurus Rex never played golf: his stubby little arms prevented him from generating significant clubhead speed, or even reaching the ground with his niblick. But what changes the lacrosse stick from a weapon to a tool is its ability to catch as well as throw—and, of course, hit.

I gotta say I was surprised to learn that William George Beers was the guy who standardized all the rules. I've watched a bunch of lacrosse matches and didn't realize there *were* any rules. It's kind of like hockey, but without the skates or camaraderie. Looks like you have to be in great shape, and I would say the second objective of the game is to score a goal. The first objective is to never have the ball. If you somehow find the ball in your stick, get rid of it right away—to a teammate, to an opponent, *at* an opponent, into the lake, whatever it takes. Otherwise, there's a pretty good chance you're going to get hit in the mouth with a lacrosse stick.

It's no coincidence that Mr. Beers was a dentist. Also no coincidence that his name is Beers.

Somewhere in here is a subtle message that, as a species, we have really let ourselves go. When you consider the First Nations would play this game with thousands of competitors, that means pretty much every guy in the tribe was included. That could never happen today. North America has a population of over five hundred million people, and fewer than two thousand guys play in the NFL. That's not exactly the whole tribe. That's less than .0005 per cent of the tribe.

And if you ever did get the whole tribe out, it wouldn't be long before heart attacks would get you back down to that same two thousand. With the development of civilization, the country gets in much better shape, but the people who live in it go the other way.

The town of Possum Lake has an unexpected connection to lacrosse. In the early 1940s, Florence Booth, pictured below, found a live hand grenade in her herb garden. She called the fire department, but he was out. She yelled to her neighbour, which she often did, but this time it was about the grenade.

Florence Booth, Local No-Nonsense Person

He was the captain of the ten-man Possum Lake lacrosse team. He gathered the team together and had them stand 100 feet apart, holding their lacrosse sticks, which created a line reaching out to the edge of town. Then he carefully picked up the grenade in his stick and hurled to the first man 100 feet away. He caught it gingerly and relayed on to the next man. And so on and so on until it got to the second-last man, but when *he* threw the grenade the pin got caught in the mesh and was pulled out by the force of throwing.

Luckily, the grenade didn't go off right away. It waited until the last man, Ernie Stubler, caught it. The ten-man lacrosse team was now a nine-man lacrosse team. Florence thanked the men and sent them on their way. Except for Ernie. He'd already left.

Ernie's Remains

Some of the residents of Possum Lake had a different application for the game of lacrosse. It was a time of horse-drawn carts, which involved horses, which involved manure on the streets. Teenagers were hired to get rid of it at the end of each week, and more often during the Christmas rush.

Not the most glamorous job in town, and the boys soon turned to lacrosse sticks to get it done. The road was clear in minutes, but the storefronts took a real beating. One outdoor café was never able to reopen, and at the doughnut shop, sales of the chocolate twist plummeted.

To see us play, go to the Book of Inventions page at redgreen.com and click on "Lacrosse."

RED SAYS: Always make a prototype. The only thing worse than a bad idea is a hundred copies of it.

GREATEST INVENTION IN THE WORLD

CANDIDATE # 7 | The Flashlight

A flashlight—or "torch," as it's called by anyone who has never held a real torch—is a portable handheld electric light source. Usually, flashlights are battery-powered with a light bulb mounted in such a way as to the direct the light in a specific direction. This allows you to locate something in the dark, but then to not see that thing on the ground in front of you, so you still stub your toe moving towards the thing you wanted.

Flashlights come in all sorts of shapes, sizes and colours. They come mounted to hard hats, and some can even be used underwater. They have regular battery-powered ones, ones that use a hand crank to charge up and, yes, they even have solar-powered ones, which I guess only work when you don't need them. Flashlights are mostly an emergency tool, so they usually end up sitting in a kitchen drawer for a couple of years. The batteries eventually die and the flashlight becomes their coffin.

When the emergency finally arrives, the power's off, it's pitch-black and the batteries are dead in your flashlight, so you can't even use it to find the new ones.

RATING: Not even close. Candidate #8 has a better chance.

MAGNETIC SHOES

Dennis Holmsworth, Lodge Member and Man on the Run

Marathon athlete and Lodge Member Dennis Holmsworth invented running shoes with magnetic inserts in the soles. He claimed they increased circulation and helped him run straighter, especially when he was heading north. To test the strength of the magnets, he ran upside down under the Mercury Creek Railway Bridge.

While Dennis's magnets held up fine, his shoe-tying skills did not. He recovered quickly and was unfortunately soon back to being his old self.

Sadly, one evening while running on the side of the highway a truckload of steel I-beams went by and Dennis was never seen again.

MUSKOL
Charles H. Coll

Charles H. Coll was born in Stellarton, Nova Scotia, on October 19, 1907. After working for Lever Brothers in Boston and Tibbetts Paints in Trenton, Nova Scotia, he started his own company in the late 1950s. His tremendous creativity even shows in the company's name—Muskol—in which the word *musk* is stuck onto his surname. I think it would have been better for him if his last name had been Ito. That way, his flagship product would've been called Muskito, and he would have been on the right track right away.

He started working on a bunch of different hunting and fishing products, and Chucky must have really liked the name he came up with, because every product he introduced was called Muskol, but with a different "flavour" depending on the animal and whether you wanted to get it to come closer or go farther away. The most successful invention of the bunch was his Muskol insect repellant. That was when he started making some serious scratch. The Coll family retained the rights to Muskol until they were sold to Schering-Plough Canada in 1982 and then to Bayer in 2015.

✳ ✳ ✳

This invention sounds like a total accident to me. Anybody whose core business is focused on hunting and fishing wants to *attract* animals, not repel them. Even the word *musk* refers to the scent female animals give off when they're in heat. There used to be a cologne called Musk that was pretty popular with teenaged boys who'd wear it as aftershave long before they needed to shave.

And hunters use deer musk or bear musk or moose musk to scent the trail to their blind. Wouldn't it be great to be an animal? No subtleties. No guesswork. The scent of the female says it all. Now that's what I call a dating service.

So instead of needing a bunch of different products, each geared to whatever animal you were trying to catch, my guess is that this guy was trying to invent a product that attracted a whole range of animals.

He knew that hunters aren't that fussy. They're out there with cold hands, cold feet and wet pants. Dammit, they wanna shoot something. They don't care what. Sometimes when they're really bored, they shoot cows or road signs. Or each other. Much better to have a bottle of something on hand that brought the wild animals and cut back on the homicides.

Charles knew that a single product that attracted everything would have a huge customer base. So I think he was trying to invent Musk-*All*, not Muskol. It probably wasn't until they started testing it that they found out what it was really good for.

Like most men, they were trying to attract something but instead found repelling came much easier.

Likely they had one guy, maybe a college student working for the summer, whom they would cover with different formulas of musk to see if any animals strolled over with lovin' on their minds. None of the formulas ever worked.

At the end of the day, this poor guy would come schlepping back to the lab covered with mosquito bites. He'd have a quick blood transfusion and then head home. Then one day, after a full eight-hour shift of no action (same as his social life), he came back with no mosquito bites. No blood transfusion required.

So the breakthrough was not in inventing the mosquito repellant, but in abandoning everything else and focusing on the fluke. A good lesson for all you inventors—you may be trying to grow the perfect flower, but your real strength may be in spreading fertilizer.

There's a basic rule at the root of Muskol or any other repellant chemical or sound or action. The rule has two parts. The first is that the animal or insect or person you are trying to repel has options—you or your property are not the only game in town. Second, that person, animal or insect must have the mental and physical capacity to analyze those options and choose the best one.

So when you're wearing Muskol, it doesn't stop the mosquito from biting. It only stops it from biting *you*. And even that doesn't work unless there's somebody or something in the area that is more appealing than you—for example, a friend, neighbour or loved one who's not wearing Muskol.

This is an important fact. If you're not alone and don't want to be alone in the near future, before you put on your Muskol, put it on your loved one first. And if there's only enough Muskol for one, she gets it. Otherwise she won't blame the mosquitos for her bites, she'll blame you.

Buster Hadfield has a stagnant pond on his property that has become a mosquito breeding ground for the entire county. He applied for a government grant to have water-bombing planes fly over the pond like they would over a forest fire, but instead of dropping water they would drop twenty thousand gallons of Muskol. Buster theorized that if each mosquito was covered in Muskol, they would repel each other and end the species.

To watch our Adventure Film on dealing with bugs, go to the Book of Inventions page at redgreen.com and click on "Repellant."

RED SAYS: Do your research before you do your project. It'll stop you from inventing things that the world already has.

PABLUM
Dr. Frederick Tisdall

I n 1931, the Mead Johnson Company came out with Pablum for the very first time. It was invented by Dr. Frederick Tisdall, Dr. Theodore Drake and Dr. Alan Brown. Three men making baby food in the '30s was a brave, brave choice. The stuff was precooked and predried and tasted like it. It was designed to fight against infant malnutrition, particularly the lack of vitamin D in babies' diets. At the same time, it was easy on the digestive system because it didn't have any lactose, nuts or eggs in it. Something you could eat with even the worst hangover.

✳ ✳ ✳

It's hard to imagine there was a time when malnutrition was a big problem in North America. It was back in the days when fat people stood out. Our generation will be remembered as the one that stamped out undereating. The brand name Pablum comes from the Latin word *pabulum*, which means "foodstuff." Similar to the word *curriculum*, which means "school stuff' or *hoodlum*, which means "guy who robs you while wearing a hood." Pablum is also a good word because it pretty much describes its flavour.

The biggest impact of Pablum is that it may have been the first "in-between" meal. It was in between food and drink. Up until that time, the idea of in-between had been limited to right and wrong, a rock and a hard place, the devil and the deep blue sea. With the creation of Pablum, which bridged the gap between one thing and another, the floodgates were opened.

Next came sushi, which is in between food and bait; hot dogs, which are in between meat and sweeping compound; a shih-tzu, which is in between a dog and a cat; the honeymoon, which is in between being single and being married; and having a government job, which is in between being unemployed and working.

A side effect of Pablum is that it proved to the world it was possible to live without teeth. This was excellent news for the entire bluegrass community. It was also very easy to digest, so you could still eat, even when you were getting over a case of the twenty-four-ounce flu.

Lodge Member and apocalyptic enthusiast Glen Friedman was inspired by Pablum. Glen had always been obsessed with the end of the world and was forever finding ways to prepare, first for the atomic fallout and then the zombie invasion. He spent a lot of long nights creating hazmat suits out of plastic shopping bags and designing a distiller that could make his own urine potable.

His older brother John came downstairs one evening to find Glen peeing into a jar with a plastic bag around his head. John suggested that since zombies ate brains, Glen would probably be safe. Glen didn't get it.

Later, Glen found the product Pablum, which he started hoarding along with condensed milk. He decided that condensed powdered food options were the way to go, so he began collecting and freezing bacon strips. When they were frozen and dry enough, he would use a belt sander to grind them down and a Shop-Vac to collect them, and then jar them and store them on shelving units. After a few months of this, Glen had quite a collection of powdered bacon.

Unfortunately, Glen had a massive gas leak in the middle of the night. And so did the house. That led to a series of explosions. First to go was the water heater, which knocked over the jars of bacon powder and reconstituted them with hot water.

When the furnace exploded, it blew out all the windows, showering the backyard with bacon bits, turning it into a giant Caesar salad. Sadly for Glen, this did not mark the end of the world, but it did mark the end of him living in his parents' basement.

Glen Friedman, Possum Lake Punk Rocker

PAINT ROLLER
Norman Breakey

Red Roller

The first paint roller was invented in 1940 by Canadian Norman Breakey, who was born in 1891. Breakey went door to door, trying to sell his invention to Toronto hardware stores. Norm was often mistaken for a door-to-door religious nut, which may be where the expression "holy roller" comes from.

After failing to attract investors, he was never able to afford a patent or even market his invention in large enough numbers to make any money at it. This was seventy years before *Shark Tank*. Competitors swooped in, made a few small changes to the paint roller's design, and were able to market it as their own invention. Breakey's paint roller got steamrollered.

One of those swoopers was Richard Croxton Adams, who held the first U.S. patent on the paint roller. He claimed that he developed it in his basement workshop in 1940 while working for the Sherwin-Williams paint company. Canadians know the real story.

✳ ✳ ✳

Hard to put a positive spin on this one. Feels like it should be called the achy-breaky, not the Norman Breakey.

This poor guy had a lot of hurdles to overcome. Too many, apparently. The biggest obstacle for any invention should be the idea itself. Breakey cleared that one. He got the hard part done, no problem. It was the "easy" stuff that did him in.

Things like protecting your intellectual property. That should be a right for everyone, not just for the people rich enough to afford the patent process. Most inventors spend all their money on building prototypes. By the time they get the thing perfected, they're broke.

Breakey's next challenge was to sell his new product to retailers by going door to door. Try to imagine how hard that would be to do. You're talking to a buyer for a hardware store who is being courted by every major hardware manufacturer and distributor in the country, and then in you walk with a weird-looking gizmo that you're asking him to buy a couple of. Kinda sounds like how it felt trying to get my TV show off the ground.

That takes a super-salesman, and my guess is Norman Breakey was not one of those.

You could say the whole project failed because Breakey needed to be a wealthy, creative, personable, yet forceful businessman who also came up with a great idea. But I don't see it that way. The only thing Breakey needed was venture capital—some person, or people, who saw the value in his invention and were prepared to become investors. An investment of ten thousand dollars would have made them all millionaires, including Breakey.

So why couldn't Breakey raise the cash? Well, it was 1940 and the world was at war, so people were cautious. Also, there would be some skepticism as to why the big paint companies hadn't already come up with this idea if it was so good. Maybe they even wondered why Breakey didn't take it to the big paint companies. Maybe Breakey's wife wondered that too. But I would say Breakey's biggest obstacle was that in Canada in 1940, there weren't a lot of people, and only a tiny percentage of that small population could be considered investors.

And as it happens, none of them was prepared to invest in a paint roller.

It's a sad story, but I guess there are two good things that came out of this mess: 1) the lesson that inventors need to team up with people who can supply the cash and expertise they don't have, and 2) thanks to Mr. Breakey, the world is a brighter place with far fewer brush marks.

As you've probably figured out already, part of the purpose of this book is to show you how you don't always need to invent the core ingredient. Sometimes all you need to do is to invent some new way of using the existing invention. Or, as in this case, creating a new way to *apply* the existing invention.

Norm didn't invent paint, but he invented a better way to get it on the walls.

So if you're getting frustrated coming up with a new product, maybe you can create a new way to apply an old product. A salt shaker that never clogs. Or a toothbrush that does all three tooth surfaces at once. Or an automated toilet brush that scrubs the bowl during every flush. The world is usually more receptive to a product that makes a good thing better rather than a product like Viagra, which probably quite often creates a supply for which there is no demand.

We featured Mr. Breakey's paint roller idea in a couple of our television shows. If we had gone another season, we would have used a paint roller to put maple syrup on waffles and sunblock on fat guys. Probably one of the reasons we weren't renewed.

To see how we used a giant paint roller, go to the Book of Inventions page at redgreen.com and click on "Roller."

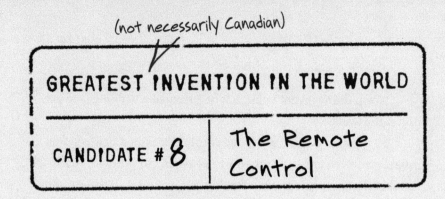

GREATEST INVENTION IN THE WORLD

CANDIDATE # 8 | The Remote Control

When I was a kid, the only way to change channels on the radio was to turn a dial on the unit itself. The TV was the same, but as it only had one channel, this was less of an inconvenience. But pretty soon we were up to ten channels, and turning the dial became an issue.

It was good in a way, because you had to be sure you really wanted to change the station before going to the trouble of dead lifting your two hundred pounds out of the La-Z-Boy to walk all the way over there. The remote control changed everything. Now you didn't have to leave the comfort of the couch to channel-flip. Just sit there and let 'er rip. And if you time it just right, you can miss whole blocks of channels just by pressing that changer really fast. You can adjust volume depending on the content of what you are watching or the sleeping status of the person beside you.

But it didn't stop there. As TVs became more and more complicated, so did the remote controls that operated them. Now you have remotes that can pause and rewind the TV. They can switch between different inputs for all that other stuff that hovers around your TV in the wall unit. There are TVs that connect to the internet and remotes that can help you browse once you get there.

And now you can get universal remotes that control all of your electronic gizmos—the DVD player, Blu-Ray, VCR, stereo system and pretty much everything else in your house. A friend of mine was trying to turn up the volume on his TV for twenty minutes before the neighbour came over, asking why his garage door kept going up and down.

It's not easy to figure out your remote anymore. It's kind of like how society has gotten. By trying to make things more convenient with tons more options and choices, they've turned every remote into an IQ test. And I'm not doing well.

RATING: Nuh-uh. Candidate #9 might be the ticket.

PIE-O-NEER

Edna Sanders, Owner of Edna's Personality Pastries: "I'd rather be flaky than crummy."

In the early 1900s, Edna Sanders lost both of her parents in a tragic murder-suicide during a euchre game in which Edna's father had decided to go alone with four nines.

Edna was an only child and inherited everything, which included a large oven and her father's floor-refinishing business (Sanders' Sanders). She decided to close down the business, move her inherited stove into the store and convert it into a bakery shop.

She was unable to get all of the sawdust off the walls and ceiling, leading to problems with the flavour and consistency of her first batch of Nanaimo bars. But over time she attracted a large number of loyal customers.

She attributed her success to her ability to create a fun, friendly atmosphere and a natural talent for making up the catchy slogans she displayed in her front window: "Praise the Lard," "This Baker Does What Other Bakers Dozen't," "Try Our Pink-eye Pies—Extra Crusty" and "If You've Got the Time, We've Got the Tarts."

Then, in the summer of 1907, Edna was hit with a problem that would change her life and career path forever.

She had been contracted to supply all the pies for Possum Lake's Centennial Celebration. They were expecting eight hundred people, and it was during a time when everyone was looking to get "their piece of the pie."

Confronted with the challenge of making a lot of pies in a short period of time, Edna decided there must be a better way. Her first step was to examine the structure and design of a conventional pie.

The first thing that struck her was the roundness of it. The second thing that struck her was the way it was sliced. The third thing that struck her was that it was now Wednesday and it taken her three full days to notice the first two things. Edna figured that the key obstacle was the pattern in which the pie was cut.

It limited each pie to a maximum of eight pieces, which meant Edna would have to make a hundred pies for the centennial. That would have drastically cut into her social life—if she had one. So instead, she toyed with the idea of slicing the pies in a different pattern.

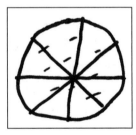

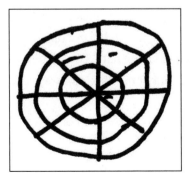
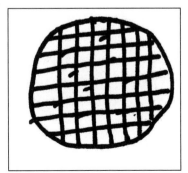

Edna soon realized that the brilliance in the conventional way of cutting a pie was that every piece got a little bit of crust with it. She needed to do more thinking. She hated that.

Then one night she awoke from a sound sleep, sat bolt upright, catching the top third of her hairstyle in the ceiling fan and sending her cats flying. But she had the answer: the problem wasn't the shape of the slices, it was the shape of the *pie*. She needed a better-shaped pie. But what shape would that be?

Edna recognized this as a geometry problem, so she went to her Grade 8 math teacher, who smiled calmly and simply said, "πr^2." Edna knew a bad joke when she heard one—pie are squared—but it got her thinking. Yes, square pies would generate more pieces and would allow more of them to fit in the oven. But how could they be cut so that every piece got some crust? It was hopeless.

Edna was so depressed that she stuck her head in the oven. She didn't turn on the gas, but still, you could tell she was upset.

It was a high-end oven, so the light came on when she opened the door. At the same time, a light went on in Edna's head. She noticed that the shape of the oven was not a square but a rectangle. Forget "pie are squared"; make it "pi are rectangular." Edna got busy collecting rectangular baking pans and laying out a cutting plan that would yield the greatest slice output while making sure every piece had a crust.

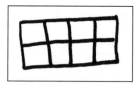

Edna knew she was on to something. The rest of the town thought she was *on* something. The interior of her oven was thirty-six inches by thirty. Using the customary ten-inch round pie pans, she could bake nine pies at once, for a total of seventy-two pieces.

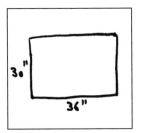

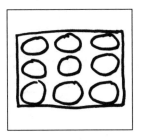

Using ten-by-six-inch rectangular pie pans, she could bake eighteen pies at once, for a total of 144 pieces, a difference of seventy-two pieces.

Do the same with two racks in the oven, and that difference increases to 216 pieces, which is another 100 per cent uptick in output.

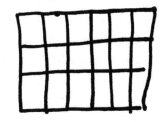

But Edna didn't stop there. She added eight more racks to the oven, which allowed her to bake 1,440 slices at once, enough for the entire celebration.

Edna was so excited that she went all over town, boasting about her creation and allowing random strangers to pat her on the back—or anywhere else they wanted to pat her. Sadly, basking in her own glory, she forgot about the pies, which were burned beyond recognition. She tried to pass them off as apple crisps, but the event was a disaster. It was the end of rectangular pies and the end of Edna's pastry shop.

Later, when asked about the failure of her pie design, Edna answered ruefully, "That's what happens when you don't cut corners."

POUTINE
Quebec

Poutine was invented in Quebec in the late 1950s or early 1960s, depending on which story you believe.

The most popular version has it being invented in 1957 at a small restaurant in Warwick, Quebec. The story goes that the restaurant had already started putting cheese curds in the fries, but one day a creative, devil-may-care truck driver named Eddy Lainesse was running late and had to eat on the road, so he ordered a side of gravy for his fries and then dumped it on top of the hot curds and fries. The owner of the restaurant, Fernand Lachance, said, "Ça va faire une maudite belle poutine!" which translates roughly to either "That will make a damn fine mess!" or "You're going to need another shirt."

Poutine has since grown into a national dish enjoyed by many people, most of whom should know better. It hasn't hurt the manufacturers of heartburn pills any, either.

✳ ✳ ✳

I guess I kinda get it. It feels like a throwback to my high school days, when one of the guys would say, "I dare you to eat that." Or maybe you're on death row and tomorrow's the big day; then I guess it would be okay to order a large poutine to chow down on as your last meal. But on a regular basis? Like, more than once a lifetime? What's goin' on here? Okay, maybe back in 1957, when we didn't know fancy words like *nutrition* or *life expectancy*, it was okay for good ol' Eddy the truck driver to assault every artery with this little heart attack in a bowl.

But not now. We know stuff now. We're not being fooled. Or at least, if we *are* being fooled, it's an inside job.

We need to wake up here, people. Let's be honest. Poutine could only happen in a country that has socialized medicine. Forget the literal translation; *poutine* is actually the French word for "goodbye." That's why most people order it "to go."

And is this all truly necessary? Do you really need to put gravy and cheese curds on top of fries? Were fries on their own just too darn healthy? That's like putting chocolate sauce and whipped cream and nuts on top of a sundae. Okay, that's a bad example, but you know what I mean.

And poutine might have been the first offender, but it's not the only one. For the last few years, KFC has been advertising a heart-stopping treat called a Double Down that's a handful of bacon sandwiched between two pieces of fried chicken. Wow. What's next? How about we stuff a turkey with a leg of lamb and then wrap the whole thing in bacon and deep-fry it in a vat of maple syrup? I know you can't wait to try that.

But on behalf of all your friends and family who'll have to carry the coffin, don't do it. Please show a little restraint, a little respect for your God-given body and a little consideration for the medics who have to rush from their homes to stand over you with a couple of paddles.

I gotta put this one in the category I call "accidental inventions." We've all heard the story of the Post-It notes coming out of creating a new glue that turned out to be useless because it never dried. Or Velcro, which was developed after the guy got a zillion burrs on his sweater. Sometimes great inventions come along when you least expect it.

The key factor is that they present themselves to people who are paying attention and thinking about what they experience and are open to opportunities. This takes an almost childlike approach to life. You can't be jaded, or you won't see anything. You can't be egotistical, or you'll reject anything that you didn't think of. You can't be close-minded, or you'll never see the value in the unexpected. So I guess you have to be immature and maybe even a bit of a dreamer to be an inventor.

That's why it's so important for an inventor to either have a steady income from a family trust or to have married well.

PULPED WOOD PAPER
Charles Fenerty

Canadian inventor and poet Charles Fenerty was born in 1821 in Nova Scotia, where, as a kid, he worked at the family lumber mill. Just stop and think about that for a minute. This guy is an inventor and a poet, and where is he working? At a lumber mill. This is why government grants were created. But despite being an artist who also had to work for a living, Charles learned a lot about the properties of different kinds of wood. He kept applying what he'd learned, and by 1844 he had come up with a way to make paper from wood pulp.

For two thousand years before that, paper had been made out of rags or cotton or hemp. They even made hemp toilet paper, which had to be a little on the rough side. I think that's why in most pictures from that era, the people are standing.

Charles came up with his invention at a time when the demand for paper was rising, and the switch to wood as a paper source was great for Canada, which has a zillion trees but not much hemp—unless you include British Columbia. When the *Acadian Reporter* did an article on Charles Fenerty, it was written on the wood pulp paper itself. Talk about inventive *and* poetic.

This is a great example of how your environment can send you down a certain path. Canada has a lot of natural resources. Minerals, freshwater, doughnuts, etc. And trees have gotta be near the top of that list. Even today, Canada has way more trees than people. No wonder we're still not out of the woods.

If every day you wake up and all you see is trees, you figure out things to do with them. In the early years, Canadians chopped down the trees to build, and then heat, log houses. They also used them to build barns and carriages and fences and silos and railway ties and bridges and whatever else they could think of.

The number of trees in this country was not lost on Mr. Fenerty. He met many of them every day at the mill. He was probably one of very few poets to work in the lumber industry, and I'm sure it wasn't easy to combine the two worlds. Very few words rhyme with *coniferous.*

And more important, if there were no women working there, what would be the point of writing poetry anyways?

So Charles was forced to channel his innovation in a different direction, and I'm guessing that finding another use for trees was his obvious first choice. Papermaking would never have been invented in Saudi Arabia, unless maybe it was sandpaper.

Chucky Boy got busy experimenting with all kinds of trees and chemicals until he got the right combination that made a pulp that was strong enough to hold together but flexible enough to be extruded in very thin sheets. It was a great invention and it changed the world, but—and I could be wrong about this, and it would be very unusual for a poet—I suspect that Charles Fenerty had no sense of smell. I mean, have you ever been through a town with a paper mill? If you had, you'd remember it, believe me. It really is a bad, bad smell and it travels well. When you stop and ask for directions to a paper mill, locals tell you, "Just follow your nose."

I can't imagine eating scrambled eggs with that smell in the air. I can't imagine a walk in the park or a baseball game or a wedding with the smell of rotting pulp burning the hair in your nostrils. The bride isn't crying tears of joy, it's just the stink in her eyes. If the groom doesn't seem to notice the smell, though, perhaps that would be a clue for her to rethink the whole situation.

But the point is—as I have hinted above—that paper mills reek. Maybe you get used to it. Maybe after you grow up on a pig farm, the paper mill is like a rose garden. I just know that when I drive past a paper mill, I make sure I do drive past, as fast as possible.

Somebody smarter than me might see it as an opportunity. Air fresheners and perfume and aftershave sales are probably through the roof in those towns. Maybe by now somebody can figure out how to make paper out of something else. Something that smells better. Chrysanthemums or licorice or something. Bad smells are tremendously underestimated (until you run into one).

These days, people put a lot of time, effort and money into looking good and feeling good. But smelling good is way more important. For a person *and* for a town. So thank you, Charles Fenerty, for pulped wood paper, and please pass the scented candle.

When I look around at the world we live in today, I can't help but think Charlie Fenerty would not have been happy. Between emails and texts and Twitter and online billing, we are quickly becoming a paperless society. It doesn't matter what paper is made of if nobody is using any. No more notepads, no cheque-books, no stationery, not even any newspapers. Even the grocery bags are plastic.

In another twenty years, the only thing left from Mr. Fenerty's invention will be toilet paper. So sad—an industry that flourished for hundreds of years, flushed down the john.

In honour of poet Charles Fenerty:

OWED TO CHARLIE

There once was a woodsman named Charlie
Who tried to make paper from barley
He said with a gulp,
"I prefer extra pulp."
It worked, but the odour was gnarly.

ROBERTSON SCREW
P. L. Robertson

P.L. Robertson was born on December 10, 1879. In his late twenties, he worked as a Canadian salesman for an American tool company. They would have preferred an American salesman, but they couldn't get any of them to move up here.

During a sales demonstration, the slot-head screwdriver he was demonstrating slipped out of the screw and cut Robertson on the hand. I'm sure he swore a couple of times—in both official languages—but it prompted him to design and patent the Robertson screw, a square-headed screw that would be more stable and way safer than the normal slot-head.

I'm thinking this might have led to a bunch of jokes about square heads and stable screws, but I can't think of any. P.L. patented the Robertson screw internationally in 1909, and his factory in Milton pumped out a ton of Robertson screws for the war effort during World War I in 1914 and its sequel in 1939. Come to think of it, there's probably a couple of square-head jokes to be made about that.

✳ ✳ ✳

Wanting to cash in on a similar device, Lodge member and all-around tool Ernie Gaither once invented a circle-head screw and screwdriver. Although at first well received, it didn't work, which is a setback for any invention. There was nothing for the screwdriver to grab on to, so it just spun around aimlessly, as did Ernie. He was disappointed, as he had already come up with a great catchphrase for the circle screwdriver: "What goes around, comes around."

Ernie Gaither, Bartender and Screwdriver Expert

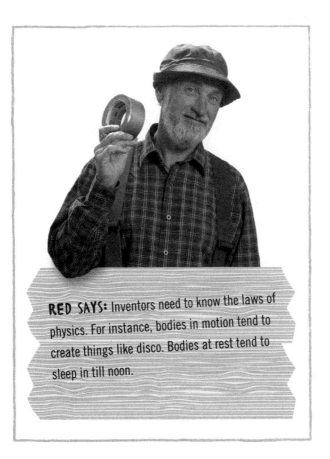

RED SAYS: Inventors need to know the laws of physics. For instance, bodies in motion tend to create things like disco. Bodies at rest tend to sleep in till noon.

SEWAGE CANNON

Doctor Ferguson, Septic
Visionary

Doctor Ferguson was born in Mercury Creek in 1914. He was not a doctor, but his parents named him Doctor because they wanted a doctor in the family. He had two siblings: a sister, Nurse Ferguson, and a younger brother, Arthroscopic Surgeon Ferguson (who later changed his name to Famous Actor Ferguson, and then finally to Waiter Ferguson).

From a young age, Doctor had been interested in human waste—he was a huge fan of his own diapers—and dedicated his life to finding a way to deal with it in an environmentally friendly way.

As an adult he would often take a picnic lunch and spend all day at the sewage plant, although even he could not do it with an egg-salad sandwich. He became familiar with the sewage treatment process and eventually realized they were going at it all wrong.

His family had a long tradition of moving away from problems rather than dealing with them, and Doctor thought this same approach could be used on sewage. If you get rid of it, you don't need to treat it. That's what the human body does.

Doctor believed the answer would come from physics, not chemistry. All he needed was an effective way to move large quantities of sewage over long distances, quickly and permanently.

When he read about the huge V-3 cannon the Germans were building in World War II, which would be powerful enough to shoot large shells from Paris to London, he knew he had his answer. Doctor began working on his sewage cannon. Not to aim at other towns, but to fire the sewage into outer space, where it would either atomize or go into a distant orbit light years away from earth. He didn't really care what happened to it, as long as it was gone and would stay gone.

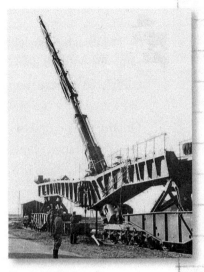

German WWII Cannon

The scientific community rejected Doctor's theory and tried to have him arrested. Doctor pressed on, claiming that sewage already existed in space and was probably a component in some of the planets. He would often point at Uranus and say, "You tell me." Doctor had been told by his Grade 10 science teacher that to put an object into orbit, it would have to reach a speed of twenty-five thousand miles an hour to be able to break free of earth's gravitational pull.

Doctor knew he'd never get that out of the cannon alone, but he believed the large quantities of methane would work as a second-stage booster rocket. Just one more of the many advantages when you're working with sewage.

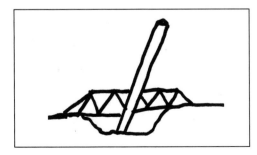

Abandoned Pipe/Cannon/
Lewd Drawing

Although reasonably well thought out when compared to his other plans, it did not go well. On September 18, 1951, Doctor completed construction of a makeshift cannon, using a truckload of explosives he borrowed from the munitions factory in Nobel, Ontario. He poured the explosives into the top end of a section of the Trans-Canada Pipeline that had fallen off a railway car and become embedded in a dried-up riverbed on the outskirts of town.

Once he had the charge compacted, he filled the rest of the pipe with raw sewage, which took contributions from everyone in town. Some gave more than others. When it was fully loaded and the area had been cleared, Doctor lit the 100-foot fuse and watched with nervous anticipation. What followed was a huge explosion that split the pipe from bottom to top while it launched a massive blob of steaming sewage into the twilight sky. Even though the methane booster rocket kicked in as expected, the load only reached a top speed of seventeen miles an hour, which was disappointingly lower than the twenty-five thousand required.

The waste did not atomize but instead formed a compacted ball of sewage that landed in the middle of the town square, where it served for the next several months as a wind direction indicator.

SNOWBLOWER

Early Snowblower

Arthur Sicard was born in Saint-Léonard-de-Port-Maurice, Quebec, on December 17, 1876. In 1894, he got the idea for a snowblower while he was looking at a farm threshing machine, which worked by using a set of revolving metal "worms" that chopped up straw and a fan that blew the straw bits up a pipe into a strawstack. If you've ever been to Quebec in the winter, you'll know why snow removal was on Arthur's mind.

But it wasn't until thirty years later, in 1924, that he got up the nerve to invest forty thousand dollars into his first machine, which was built by hand and patented. Arthur called it the Sicard Snow Remover Snowblower. Not what you would call a catchy name, but it allowed him to start up Sicard Industries in Sainte-Thérèse, Quebec. Although the snowblower was a huge success for Sicard, the shovel industry was hit hard and forced to move its focus from homeowners to cattle ranchers and gravediggers.

❋ ❋ ❋

 As usual, there's a lot more here than meets the eye. This invention did not start on paper or even as an idea. There wasn't a lot of research or even theory involved with this baby. Most of the work had already been done by the guy who invented the thresher.

What Mr. Sicard really did was to find a different use for an existing, and proven, technology. And more power to him. He saved plenty of time and money by repurposing rather than creating. It was unfortunate for the thresher folks that they didn't do this themselves, and fortunate for Mr. Sicard that the patent board didn't see it as an infringement on an existing patent. Maybe the thresher gang was busy separating the wheat from the chaff and didn't have the time or interest to separate the original from the copy.

A good lesson for all of you inventors out there: you're way better off to find something that already exists and works, and then find a way to use it in a completely different application that is not covered by their patent. Like, say, using a clothes dryer as a popcorn maker. Or a Ping Pong table as an adjustable bed.

(To see how we used a clothes dryer as a popcorn maker, go to the Book of Inventions page at redgreen.com and click on "Popcorn" [Ep. #193—Sausage Envy—Tip]. To see how we used a Ping Pong table as an adjustable bed, go to the same place and click on "Ping Pong" [Ep. #10—The Lost Toupee—Corner].)

The other and way more important difference between the snowblower and the thresher is what they do with the material they're handling. The thresher blows the straw into a wagon or a hopper. The snowblower just blows the snow away—to somewhere else. You don't care where it goes, as long as it's off your driveway.

But maybe your neighbour cares. Maybe he thinks that when you blow your snow at his house, it's the same as him having to shovel his driveway *and* yours. How long do you think he's going to wanna do that? Not long, that's how long. And what's he gonna do? Well, he's not gonna come over and make a big deal out of it. He's not gonna start an argument or poison your dog. He's gonna take a hard look at your snowblower and then he's gonna go down to the hardware store and buy one about three times the size. Game on. He who snowblows last, snowblows best.

Again, kudos to Sicard—he created a product that by its very annoying nature generates more sales of said product. It's called the domino effect, and it works for snowblowers, cars, guns—and breast implants.

Perhaps the most dangerous of all of the messages carried by a snowblower is the disturbing idea that if you have something on your property that you want to get rid of, it's not necessary to dispose of it safely. Instead, you can just toss it—into the street, into your neighbour's yard, into the lake. Until the snowblower came along, these were all unacceptable options. In reality, a snowblower just throws snow at other people better and faster than you could on your own. It would be like saying that using a potato gun as a pooper scooper is okay when just throwing the stuff wouldn't be.

And sure, I know you're going to say it's only snow, but that's because you don't have a gravel driveway. The truth is, powerful snowblowers can throw a lot more than snow—rocks, logs, car parts, garden gnomes. House window sales are up over 500 per cent since the invention of the snowblower. That's not a coincidence.

In the middle of last winter, when satellite reception at the Lodge was not working because of a pretty big difference between the amount paid and the amount owed, a bunch of the guys decided to attack the boredom head on by designing and then building the world's largest and most powerful snowblower. (Actually, I said that wrong. Their style is not to design, but to just build. The design part happened along the way.) The first step was to get our hands on the largest double auger we could find. The output of any snowblower is tremendously affected by how much snow it can take in. We decided to go with two spiral slides from the park in the middle of town. Kids don't go to the park in the winter anyway.

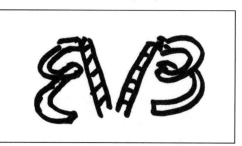

Next, we needed a small auger to raise the snow inside the snowblower. We decided to use the posthole digger the county uses for telephone poles. Nobody puts up telephone poles in the winter anyway.

With these sizes of augers, we were going to be supplying a lot of snow, so we needed a big, big fan to handle that load. I know bankrupt airlines don't have garage sales very often, but when they do, you can pick up a decommissioned turboprop real cheap. Especially if it's never going to be airborne—well, at least not on purpose.

The last and probably least important component was the vehicle on which to mount all the gear. It needed to be big and heavy with a lot of road clearance. We decided to go with a used school bus. It was strong enough to hold the mounting brackets, with a big enough engine to drive the augers, and with a Lodge member in every seat, we could get a GVW of over twenty thousand pounds. Nobody uses a school bus in the winter anyway.

We did the first—and last—trial run of our Super Snowblower on a quiet Saturday in February after a big snowstorm. We didn't tell anybody what we were doing, but once the turboprop fired up, it was pretty hard not to be noticed. We picked the Fifth Line as our test road, because there's not much traffic and, thanks to its location between Possum Lake and the escarpment, it gets a lot of heavy snow-drifts. We decided to do our first pass at a fairly good clip because if the bus got stuck, we'd never get it back out. We were doing about fifty klicks when we hit the first snowdrift. Every window of the bus was immediately covered with hard-packed snow. That was a setback, but we decided to keep the pedal to the metal with the heater on and eventually the snow on the windows would melt.

We could tell by the straining noises on the machinery that we were moving a lot of snow. None of us could tell you how far we got down the Fifth Line, but the arresting officer estimated it at around three miles. If we had it to do over (which the judge has assured us we won't), we would have aimed the exhaust chute away from the centre of town. Our five-minute drive-by has gone into the record books as the most severe snowstorm in the history of our town. And it wasn't just snow we were throwing. In the end, the mayor offered to drop charges if we shovelled everyone's driveway, paid to have the road resurfaced and fished the roadkill out of the lake.

If you want to see another way I use a snowblower, go to the Book of Inventions page at redgreen.com and click on "Snowblower."

RED SAYS: Before creating any invention, you should come up with an excuse—or at least an explanation—as to why it didn't work and why you are now living in an abandoned vehicle.

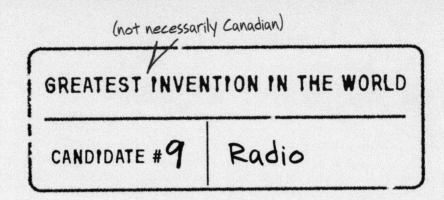

(not necessarily Canadian)

GREATEST INVENTION IN THE WORLD

CANDIDATE #9 | Radio

In the late nineteenth century, an Italian inventor named Guglielmo Marconi started working with radio waves to try to make a wireless telegraph system that could be turned into a commercial business. For it to work, the signal needed to travel a long distance, which Marconi was able to do by grounding both the receiver and transmitter (and maybe his teenaged daughter) and raising the antenna height. Let's give him the benefit of the doubt and assume that raising the antenna was more or less a given.

Before long, Marconi was able to transmit and receive radio waves up to two miles. That was great news for anyone who lived near him, but pretty much meaningless to everyone else. Guglielmo knew that he needed to be able to market this thing to people who were more than two miles apart. He kept experimenting, and on December 12, 1901, he successfully transmitted a wireless telegraph signal from England to St. John's, Newfoundland. Now you're talkin'—or should I say, now you're *typin'*. In any case, the seeds of modern radio had been planted. This meant the writing was on the wall for vaudeville, but fortunately many of the performers couldn't read.

RATING: You know it can't possibly be radio, because it was totally eclipsed by television. There's a hint about Candidate #10.

SNOWMOBILE
Joseph-Armand Bombardier

Born on April 16, 1907, in Valcourt, Quebec, Joseph-Armand Bombardier invented the snowmobile. It was born out of the tragedy of his son not being able to receive crucial medical attention during a blizzard.

Not wanting anybody else to have to suffer that kind of loss, Bombardier designed a vehicle that could move through heavy snow. It had a caterpillar-track system that used a rubber-toothed wheel and a rubber-and-cotton track that wrapped around the back wheels.

It had pretty much the same design they still use today. A lot of us owe plenty to Monsieur Bombardier.

As we say at the Lodge, "Those who can ski, do. Those who can't, SkiDoo."

✳ ✳ ✳

I think this is a great invention because it saves lives and helps people deal with their environment, but mainly because I'm a man. And when you're a man, you believe anything that can be done, can be done better with an internal combustion engine.

We like the power, we like the noise, we like the smoke, we even like the smell. Even sex would be better if we could somehow strap on a two-cycle reciprocating engine. I'm not exactly sure how it would work, but the thought of it puts a smile on my face.

For hundreds of years men rode horses and paddled canoes and walked. We're done with that. What's the point of going fishing if you don't have a two-hundred-horsepower Evinrude strapped to the transom? Hells Angels don't ride bicycles. Why chop down a tree with an axe when you have a forty-eight-inch chainsaw with a supercharger? Man is the only animal in nature that runs towards an explosion. We love 'em. That's the appeal of internal combustion engines—you get a thousand explosions a minute. When we hear them, we're moved both physically and emotionally.

Men like moving. It makes them tougher targets and allows them to get away from the results of their mistakes. Electric cars may be the wave of the future, but they'll never be able to replace the thrill of a big-block V-8 roaring to life. You've only got one life to live—live it peeling rubber.

The most interesting aspect of the snowmobile is that it is really just one of three very similar machines. Like a good Thanksgiving dinner, the ability to put a belt in motion is the primary engineering component for all three. Monsieur Bombardier devised his machine to have a drive roller at the front and an idler roller at the back, and then a series of bogey wheels to position the track so that it would carry the weight of the vehicle to the ground, which provided traction and propulsion.

If you take the same design but have the front and rear rollers mounted on brackets, those brackets would carry the weight of the machine. The belt would have no traction and no propulsion, and instead of a snowmobile, you would have a treadmill.

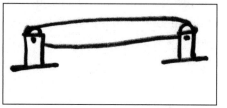

If you then take off the short belt and replace it with one a hundred feet long or more, by simply removing the bogey wheels and adding more idler rollers, then instead of a treadmill, you would have a conveyor belt.

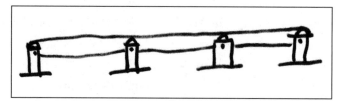

Doesn't it make more sense to combine all three of these into one? Not necessarily, but we're going to do it anyway.

The first step is to get a section of roller bed like the kind they used to use in North American factories back when North America had factories. You can get a used one pretty cheap because it's expensive to ship them to China. The longer the better, but I would say fifty feet would be a minimum.

You'll probably have to pick it up in sections, as there's only so much you can safely balance on the roof of a minivan. When you put the sections together it needs to be pretty strong, so don't spare the duct tape. Once you've got it all connected, check all the rollers to make sure they're all lubed up and ready to roll.

Next, you'll need a belt long enough to go around the rollers. That would be a little over a hundred feet. Preferably made of rubber or canvas, but in a pinch you could go to an upholstery shop and get a roll of Naugahyde. You may have to patch together a few pieces to make it work, so I suggest you either double-stitch 'em or use safety pins. You might think a bunch of suspenders clipped together would work instead, but I can tell you from experience, you would be dead wrong.

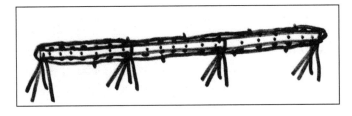

The next step is pretty easy. Pick up your snowmobile and put it on one end of the belt. Tie the skis tightly to the supporting legs of the roller bed with tie-down straps.

Now you have an instant conveyor belt able to convey whatever it is you're trying to convey. And possibly a little more than that. Just start up the snowmobile, put it in gear (not reverse) and you'll be able to vary the speed from fast to really fast. And it's even easier to make it a treadmill—just get on it. In fact, you and your friends can all exercise at the same time.

(On a safety note—make sure you're the one closest to the snowmobile. That way, if things go wrong, you'll have lots of people to land on.)

And to make it into a snowmobile, just untie the tie-down straps, put it in gear (again, not reverse) and let 'er rip. Talk about fun.

To see what Possum Lodge member Blair Cobden did with his snowmobile, go to the Book of Inventions page at redgreen.com and click on "Snowmobile."

SOLAR PANEL

Sven Boldarov, Lodge Member and "Go-To" Idea Guy

Although the solar panel was not a Canadian invention, it does have a Canadian connection. In the late '50s and early '60s, Northwest Territories resident and Possum Lodge member Sven Boldarov got hooked on the concept of solar panels but was looking for an invention that would work better in the north, where it's night for so much of the year.

After reading a couple of pamphlets and thinking for a minute or two, Sven decided to invent "lunar panels." His plan was to arrange a substantial number of photovoltaic cells in series on a large grid, in order to harness the light from the moon. He started by stapling seven thousand bicycle reflectors to the roof of his barn.

Sven didn't have equipment sensitive enough to read the actual voltage achieved, but he said it hovered around zero. No one in the scientific community questioned that. Sven was undaunted, which is unfortunate. He gave a press conference where he explained the disappointing results by reminding the naysayers that the moon is tricky because it has various phases and some nights it isn't there at all. There were no questions.

Sven decided to massively expand the number and size of his lunar panels by covering every horizontal surface on his property with reflectors. He rented airspace from his neighbours so that he could suspend large, horizontal, reflector-filled billboards above their land. He collected the energy for a month and stored it in a huge grid of rechargeable camera batteries. At the end of the month, when he turned the juice on, the batteries contained enough power to briefly illuminate the indicator light above the on/off switch. Sven vowed he would never give up, but his wife reminded him of another vow he'd made and he immediately dismantled all the lunar panels and went back to his accounting job.

We can only speculate as to what the future holds in the area of converting the sun's rays to usable electric power. Research is already in place to develop an automobile paint that contains billions of microscopic photovoltaic cells capable of generating enough power to run the vehicle. Next they'd put it into asphalt so that every road and parking lot would become a source of electricity. If this same technology could be injected into the bloodstream at the molecular level, it could use the body's own circulatory system to embed these receptors in the human skin, effectively making every person a living solar panel. Power to the people.

Rechargeable batteries could be concealed in their shorts and receive electrical energy through a USB port located somewhere in the rectal area. Suddenly bald guys would be electric, string bikinis would help save the planet, and fat people would be able to power their own soft-ice-cream machines. Kids everywhere would rejoice when sunscreen was banned.

And if you really open your mind up, we could use the other planets in our solar system as energy sources. All we'd need to do is cover them with panels and then find a way to send the power back to earth. Maybe we could email it. Or if that's too expensive, we could text it.

RED SAYS: Inventing a time-saving device that comes with a three-hundred-page instruction manual is not progress.

SONAR
Reginald Fessenden

A lot of people were shocked and stunned by the *Titanic* tragedy of 1911, but Reginald Fessenden of East Bolton, Quebec (see also page 7), decided not to stay that way. He got to work on inventing the Fessenden oscillator. What a thrill it must have been to have an oscillator named after you.

This machine could detect underwater objects, such as icebergs or submarines, by sending out sounds and then picking up their echoes. In recent times it has also come in handy for finding snowmobiles at the bottom of the lake. In 1915, ten British H-class submarines were launched from Montreal. Every one of 'em had a Fessenden oscillator, and they weren't afraid to use them.

We're not exactly sure when the name got changed to sonar, but the story around the Lodge is that there was already a product with a similar name to the Fessenden oscillator and it was already on sale in many adult stores. Almost everyone in the navy was familiar with that product, so to avoid confusion and embarrassing injury, they started calling this new gadget sonar.

I'm not absolutely sure how sonar works. On the other hand, I don't know how a coffee machine works, either, but I can still drink the stuff. Maybe sonar measures the time it takes for the echo to come back. I know sound travels at 1,100 feet per second (faster if you yell), so if the bottom of the ocean was 5,500 feet down, the echo might take ten seconds to bounce back (five seconds to get there, five more to get back). But when you come to an underwater mountain or shipwreck or a big hole, the echo would take longer or shorter and you could figure out the size and shape of the object by converting the different time results to differences in size and structure.

This is just my guess as to how sonar works. I suppose I could have looked it up, but I'm way too busy writing this book to do any research for it. I'm also thinking sonar is probably obsolete by now, with all the high-powered laser beams and robot subs they have these days. It's hard to invent any kind of technology that lasts long. You're better to focus on creating new things for the human race. The human body has not had a major design change since Adam coughed up a rib.

The Hedgeworth twins of Mercury Creek had always been fascinated with sound. They would sit in the back of the class-room and make experimental noises by cupping their hands and

Hedgeworth Twins, Shared a Lodge Membership

squeezing them under their armpits. They were able to tell how far the teacher was from them by how long till they heard the scream.

What soon became known as the Hedgeworth cheer got them a lot of laughs, very few dates and an occasional trip to the principal's office. Naturally, they were interested in the theory behind sonar and were looking to find other applications that used the same science—the ability to identify the shape and size of unseen objects just by measuring the time it took for sound waves to bounce back. They would often go downtown with a stopwatch and yell at tall buildings to determine how far away they were.

They abandoned this technique because there were too many variables. The volume of the yell, the hearing of the listener, the speed and direction of the wind all gave the boys a wide range of results from the same test. The problem was made worse by the fact that people could just look at a building and have a pretty good idea of how far away it was. Also, nobody cared, which was a setback.

So the Hedgeworths decided to abandon the approach of using sound and echo, which had already been perfected by Fessenden. Instead, they experimented with solid objects that they would bounce off random surfaces and use the return rate to determine the distance and form of those surfaces. They started by using tennis balls, but found them no good for long throws and really vulnerable to wind conditions.

Ultimately, they went with an India rubber ball, which gave them much more reliable data. One brother would put on a blindfold and allow the other brother to hurl the India rubber ball at a surface. The ball would return at speed and strike the blindfolded brother somewhere in the chest area. This process would be repeated until the entire surface had been scanned. Then the first brother would remove the blindfold and by merely looking at the size, pattern and level of discolouration of the bruises, he was able to deduce the shape and relative distance of the surface the ball had been bouncing off of. Onlookers were able to make several more deductions, none of them flattering.

The brothers went to the municipal office to apply for a patent, but instead were sent to the Ministry of Health, where they eventually received the psychiatric care they so desperately needed. They bounced back in no time.

STANDARD TIME
Sir Sandford Fleming

Sir Sandford Fleming was born in Scotland in 1827 and grew up there, but by the time he was eighteen, his family had moved to Canada. Most people, present company excluded, knew he was famous for helping create the Royal Society of Canada and the Royal Canadian Institute and played a big part in designing a lot of Canada's Intercontinental Railway. But his biggest achievement was establishing standard time. Somebody had to do it. It was time.

After missing a train in Ireland in 1876, Sir Sandford got the idea for a single twenty-four-hour clock that the whole world could use. I might have suggested not going out drinking in Ireland the night before an early morning train ride, but what do I know? In 1879, he proposed that this world clock be linked to the anti-meridian of Greenwich (the 180th meridian). Fleming suggested that standard-time zones should be used locally, but all would be so many hours plus or minus what he called "Cosmic Time." Far out, man.

✳ ✳ ✳

Standard time was obviously a great invention, but I gotta tell ya, this one is a head-scratcher. According to the history books, people started telling time using sundials and obelisks around 2,000 BCE. Sir Sandford finally got the process standardized in 1879. To me, that means that humans managed to be unbelievably stupid for almost four thousand years. What is the point of telling time if we don't synchronize our watches? "I'll meet you at the pub at eight thirty." "Okay, what time do you have now?" "Three fifteen." "That's weird, my watch says 11:27." "Nope. It's three fifteen." "Tell you what, I'll meet you at the pub at sundown." "Done." "And don't forget, they close at 2:09."

I'm prepared to cut a little slack for those who were using sundials, because the sun shines a little differently everywhere you go. But when they switched to something with a pendulum or a mainspring, there's really no excuse. It's actually worse than no excuse, it's stupid. I think they knew something was wonky. They tried to fix it with a big clock in the middle of town that everybody could see and set their watches to, but the guy who set that big clock had no idea what time it was. So it wasn't a perfect solution.

Until Sir Sandford fixed this mess, there should only have been two times of day—light and dark. Anything in between was a flat-out guess. They called it a watch, but it was really just a bracelet.

And can you imagine the guys who had to deal with standard time when it first came out? The boss could finally prove that you were actually late for work. Or worse, your wife could do the same for when you got home. I'm guessing that was a rude wake-up call for a lot of men who were used to getting off by just setting their own watches differently throughout the day. That's why some guys like the Lodge so much—we have basically reverted to hunger pains and possum squeals to tell us what time it is.

Throughout history, time has been one of the most confusing elements. I personally have been exposed to many conflicting theories on the subject. Time flies. Time drags on. Time stands still. Time waits for no man (but almost every woman). Time is of the essence. Take as much time as you need. It's time. It's not time. You need a timeout. Time's up. Time starts now. Not this time. Maybe next time. Don't do what you did last time.

Maybe Sir Sandford managed to get everybody in the world on the same schedule, but I don't believe you can completely standardize time because, as my soulmate Albert Einstein said, "Time is relative." I agree with that. Time goes much slower when you spend it with your relatives. Nobody can convince me that time travels at the same speed when you're enjoying a romantic interlude as it does when you're having a root canal. I have more theories on the subject, but I'm out of time.

Rory Ipkiss, Lodge Member with Time On His Hands

Lodge member Rory Ipkiss tried to revert the town back to sundial technology back in the '80s. He claimed that the sundial was more accurate, more energy-efficient and had stood the test of time in terms of reliability.

One night he set a massive sundial in the main town square of Possum Lake. Rory ingeniously positioned the dial so that the shadow fell on his office building at 9 a.m., the deli at noon and the bar at 5:30 p.m. Best of all, there was no shadow once the sun went down, so he never missed curfew coming home.

Possum Lake agreed to try the sundial method, but three days later there was a cloudy day and none of the kids came in after recess. The sundial was toppled, as was Rory's good name. He spent the rest of his life living in the shadow of his great idea.

To see my patent-pending beer bottle clock, go to the Book of Inventions page at redgreen.com and click on "Clock."

SUPERMAN
Joe Shuster

Joe Shuster was born in Toronto on July 10, 1914. Cousin to Frank Shuster of the comedy team of Wayne and Shuster, Joe grew up in Toronto, which is the model he used for Superman's fictional city, Metropolis. Later, Joe moved to Cleveland and met Jerry Siegel. The two guys worked together to create the Superman character. So Superman is (kind of) Canadian, which explains why he's so polite. On the other hand, Wonder Woman is American. Somebody should do a movie where they get married and argue about which side of Niagara Falls to spend their honeymoon on. Or not.

✳ ✳ ✳

I can't speak for the rest of the world, but I gotta believe Superman is the most famous superhero in North America. As a kid, I used to read Superman comics written and illustrated by Shuster and Siegel. I can remember seeing their names on the cover. Comics were popular with kids way back then. They were in colour when TV was still black and white. In fact, our first TV was *green* and white. But even so, my strongest memories of the character are from watching the original *Superman* television series starring George Reeves.

I don't know if it was because I was a kid or because society was different back then, but we never questioned anything. We just accepted whatever anyone did or said. Looking back at it now, I see a lot of problems with Superman's character and habits.

Let's start with his glasses. Everybody who worked at the *Daily Planet* knew that Clark Kent was a good friend of Superman's, but it never occurred to them that he *was* Superman. Yes, it was partly the suit, but the main way he disguised himself was by putting on glasses. And nobody ever caught on. He had the same build as Superman, the same head, the same hair, the same face, but once those glasses went on, it was a whole new ball game.

Wanted criminals spend thousands of dollars on plastic surgery and hair transplants and who knows what, all so that nobody will ever recognize them. Apparently, all they had to do was put on a pair of glasses.

The next black hole of logic was the phone-booth change room. Whenever there was trouble, Clark Kent would zip into a phone booth and change into Superman. He'd step in as Clark, wearing glasses and a suit and tie, and come out as Superman, with no glasses but with blue tights highlighting his big *S*. Some of you out there may have never seen a phone booth, but I can tell you they had windows, top to bottom, on all four sides. If there was a guy in there taking his pants off, somebody's gonna be calling the cops.

Next issue, what did Superman do with Clark's clothes? He never came out of the phone booth with them. Were they just piled on the floor in the corner? His suit? His shoes? His socks? His keys? What about his wallet? Superman never came out with a wallet—everybody would have noticed the bulge in his tights. What happened to that stuff? Did Superman go back for it? I doubt it. Nobody paid attention when Clark stepped into a phone booth and came out as Superman, but the other way around would have drawn a crowd for sure.

My guess is that Superman just abandoned those clothes. That means Clark Kent was going through at least one suit a week. Pretty tough on a newspaper reporter's salary. One more lingering question for me: Where was the red cape? When Clark was dressed in his suit with the Superman outfit underneath, where was the cape? Tucked down into the back of his pants? Sitting in a roll on top of his shoulders? Wouldn't that give him a hump? It had to be in there somewhere, but where? So many mysteries.

Then there were his superpowers. "Faster than a speeding bullet." "Able to leap tall buildings in a single bound." Now hang on a minute. If a guy is faster than a speeding bullet, why would he ever need to leap tall buildings? Way faster to just run around them. And why would he have to bound at all? Flying, sure, I can see the value in that, but bounding is pretty useless.

And of course, Superman was bulletproof. Every show, some bad guy would shoot at him. (Always in the chest, for some reason. If I was a bad guy, I would see if a bullet would bounce off Supe's forehead.) Then, after all six bullets had bounced off him, the bad guy would throw the gun at Superman. Hey buddy, if the bullets didn't work . . . Just saying.

And then there's the X-ray vision. That was a pretty edgy superpower. Every teenaged boy in America would have some fun with that one. I don't think too many women wear lead underwear. Although in the '50s, they came close.

I have to say, though, that the addition of kryptonite was brilliant. Superman having an Achilles heel was a stroke of genius that allowed the bad guys to temporarily get the upper hand. I'm not exactly sure how they got their hands on kryptonite. I've never seen it on eBay. But it was another one of those things we just accepted.

And there's the whole role model issue—"fighting for truth, justice and the American way." Superman was presented as having a moral code as high as the buildings he could bound over. The kind of person every boy would want to grow up to be like. Well, let's take a closer look. You've got a guy in his mid-thirties who's not married, no kids, doesn't have a girlfriend, makes hardly any money and lives alone in some apartment that was so bad they never showed it on TV. If it wasn't for the flying, bounding and citizen's arrests, this guy would just be another loser with X-ray vision.

The other characters didn't come off much better. Lois Lane was in love with Superman. Where did she think that relationship was going? Was she hoping to marry him one day and have a houseful of superkids? It's hard to find a house with a lead-lined bathroom. But Lois never smartened up. And neither did we.

And over and over again, Jimmy Olsen sent out the message that you can be breathtakingly stupid, but as long as you're affable you will always have a job. In my experience, the only other guy who's been able to pull that one off is me.

Superman didn't really become Superman until Joe Shuster went to the States and teamed up with Jerry Siegel. Superman feels to me more like an American than a Canadian.

Makes you wonder how the character would have been different if Shuster had stayed in Canada and made his character more Canadian. For starters, he'd probably be called Averageman—a little shy, a good guy who just wanted a normal life and was really, really polite in both official languages. The iconic image would be of him standing in line at a Tim Hortons with his hands in the pockets of an off-the-rack snowmobile suit with a lower case *a* (pronounced "eh") embroidered on the chest.

Instead of taking his glasses off before a fight, he'd put them on so nobody would take a swing at him. He would have X-ray vision, but would never use it because it's none of his business. His other superpowers would have been humility, empathy and the ability to apologize faster than the Avro Arrow.

Even though he was pretty strong and smart in reality, Averageman would pretend to be weaker and dumber so as not to make the other guy feel bad. That would be his default position for dealing with confrontation and negotiating international trade deals. His only weakness would be the Canadian dollar, and even when he had to beat the bad guys, there was always the risk that he would get killed on the exchange rate.

To find out how you married guys can be superheroes, go to the Book of Inventions page at redgreen.com and click on "Superhero."

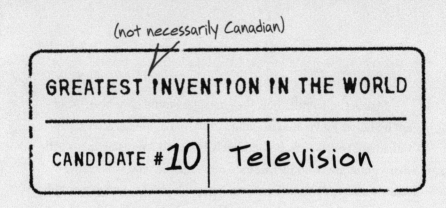

Television was invented by a whole whack of people in the early twentieth century. They all knew there'd be a zillion advantages to anything that could transmit both sound and moving pictures. What a great way to share news, sports, entertainment— and reality shows. Up until the invention of television, families gathered on their couches in the evening, staring at a blank wall. Television been called a "vast wasteland," but today it provides a huge range of things to watch. It's up to the viewer to decide.

People like choice. There's a reason Baskin and Robbins has thirty-one flavours. Some television is an important eye on the world. Some is just filler. You choose. I'm not exactly sure where my show fit in, but we used to promote it by saying, "When you've already wasted most of your life, what's another half-hour?"

RATING: Nope. Ha ha, fooled ya. But the real deal is coming up. Last chance to take a guess.

AND THE WINNER IS (on page 228)

SYNCHRONIZED SWIMMING
Synchronized Swimming

Peggy Seller, First Lady of Synchronized Swimming

Peggy Seller was the driving force behind the creation of synchronized swimming as the sport we know today. Or at least some of us know today. Or at least some of *you* know today.

A really good swimmer herself and a respected member of the Royal Life Saving Society, Peggy not only wrote the rules for the first provincial championship, but she also won the event easily. I'm sure that's a coincidence. It was held in 1924 at the YWCA in Montreal. The very next year, it became a national event, and Peg went on to win four straight national championships. Four more coincidences.

Over the next fifty years she worked really hard to see the small sport grow in Canada and worldwide, writing and rewriting rule books (when she lost?), standardizing methods of judging competitions, forming various governing bodies and organizing demonstrations of the sport. She was really into this thing. This work culminated in 1984, when synchronized swimming was adopted as an official Olympic event. Peg was inducted into Canada's

Sports Hall of Fame in 1966. Some of the swimmers were late arriving to the ceremony, as they had synchronized their routines but not their watches.

✳ ✳ ✳

 Something's not quite right about the above description. I'm sure it's factual and accurate and all that, but it just seems odd to me that Ms. Seller is reported to be the winner of all of those events. It's synchronized swimming. How can you win that on your own? Shouldn't there be at least one other winner? Your partner, for example?

Or did Peggy leave a little loophole when she wrote the rules? A loophole that said if you had created the sport, you were allowed to compete alone? Peggy would be the only qualifier and would have a pretty good chance of winning. You can't get more synchronized than that. I'm sure there's a logical and correct explanation, but I like mine better.

I guess the biggest challenge is the synchronization part. I can't think of an animal less likely than human beings to do things exactly the same way. Bees, sure. Ants, yes. Lemmings, no doubt. But humans? We hardly ever do anything the same way twice on our own, much less do it the same way somebody else does. So when we do things exactly together, we are fighting our own nature. We gotta overcome our own unpredictability.

That's a big ask. Unpredictability has always worked well for us. It makes it harder for wild animals to track us, and more important, it makes us more interesting to women. And for those of us who got cheated on the handsomeness quotient, more interesting is all we got. There's also a tinge of redundancy to copying others. If I'm just gonna do what you do, why am I here? You don't need two people to get the mail. And you sure don't need two people in perfect step with matching arm motions to go and get the mail. That'll just freak out the neighbours.

So the wonder of synchronized swimming—and for me there are plenty—is that these people have focused their skill and their training on becoming less human and more robotic. A living testament to the idea that "we're all in this together."

The concept of synchronized swimming is kind of like a university study on what it's like to live in a society. There are leaders and there are followers. The leaders see themselves as smart. They don't pay attention to what the other people are doing. They set their own paths, make their own rules, march to the beat of a different drummer. The followers see themselves as stupid. They're not smart enough to make any decision. They look for a leader and then do what they're told. The leaders have power and fame and dignity.

The followers originally had none of those. Then slowly, over time, the followers began to add order to their following. Armies started marching in step, jet fighters started flying in formation, pipers and drummers began playing the same notes and rhythms while doing the same things with their hands and feet. Not to mention *Riverdance*. Synchronized swimming is just another form of the same behaviour. An activity that adds dignity and skill to the lowly art of being a follower.

It's easy to just follow willy-nilly with no set pattern or bound-aries. To follow by exactly mirroring what the leader is doing is really, really hard. Probably harder than leading. But still not difficult enough for Peggy, so she made people do it underwater.

In the early days, she probably should have called it synchro-nized drowning. So thank you, Peggy, for giving all of us followers something to be proud of. You have proven to the world that it's better to be a perfect follower than an imperfect leader. But I still think you should have shared the trophy.

No Possum Lodge member has ever participated in synchronized swimming, although Buster Hadfield says he dated twins one time.

Local swimming enthusiast Becky Morecki won three Port Asbestos city championships before it was discovered that her partner was actually a strategically placed full-length mirror.

Rebecca Morecki

THE THEORY OF NOTHING

Cecil Hodgkiss, Part-Time Philosopher/
Full-Time Distributor of Advertising Flyers

Historically, the Possum Lake area
has always had a shortage of
intellectuals. I blame a combination of heredity and logic. People
aren't usually smarter than their
parents, and even by some fluke of
nature when we did get a smart
person, they tended to move away.
So it made us all proud when the
community labelled Cecil
Hodgkiss as "the smart guy with
the funny suits who handed out coupons at the liquor store."

Cecil pretty much had an opinion on everything and came
across as superior. A lot of it was his accent, which was either
British or Australian or German—or maybe he was just always
eating a hard candy when he spoke. He also talked really fast, like
a car speeding down a bumpy road so that maybe it'd help him
over the rough spots.

He usually was the centre of any discussion, because he could
talk far longer than any normal person could listen. He had a lot
of theories about science and history and women and had
experienced quite a bit of all of them, except for women. He did

claim to have dated a sasquatch, but we all think it was Moose Thompson's sister.

His big party-piece speech was what he called the Theory of Nothing. He started by separating the four categories of things— something, anything, everything and nothing. He had noticed that most people want something, some will settle for anything, a few had to have everything, and a very, very small number of people wanted nothing.

Cecil also noticed that this last group, the ones who wanted nothing, were the happiest and generally most satisfied with life. That got him to focus on the power of nothing and to make it the centrepiece of his argument. He said the world needed to have a reversal in definitions. The normal thinking was that the concept of nothing was seen as the absence of anything, just like darkness was seen as the absence of light.

Cecil wanted to switch those around. Light was the absence of darkness, and anything was the absence of nothing. He said it made "nothing" sound more important because it was saying the absence of it was a bad thing.

Cecil became a huge fan of nothing, and his income backed that up. He said that things wear out and break. Nothing doesn't. "Nothing ever changes," he would say and then give that wink that made people want to smack him into the middle of next week. He believed that nothing was important—or, as he put it, "Nothing matters," but no wink this time. When people questioned his knowledge on the topic, Cecil would get mad and shout, "I know nothing!" And for anyone who was still listening—or still reading, in this case—Cecil would take his theory into the ionosphere. Beyond the ionosphere. Outer space, actually.

That was the head office of nothing. Space is made up mostly of nothing, and here's the kicker: it's infinite. Nothing is the only resource in the universe that we will never run out of. Shouldn't we be working with that? Shouldn't we be finding things to do with nothing?

Let's examine its properties. It has no atoms, no molecules, no gravity, no gases, no energy of any kind. That may seem hopeless to us, but not to Cecil, who also seems hopeless to us. Cecil decided what outer space—and, by definition, nothing— was best suited for: storage. A place to keep something or any- thing, or in fact, big enough to store *everything*. And it would never rot, spoil, age, rust, evaporate, fall over or roll away. It would all be frozen in time because, as Cecil would remind us, "Nothing lasts forever."

At this point in his presentation, Cecil tried to expand the application to use the nothingness of outer space to quarantine diseases and keep his wife's shoes, but by then the authorities had arrived and most of his speech was muffled by the straitjacket.

TRIVIAL PURSUIT AND BALDERDASH
Chris Haney and Scott Abbott

C hris Haney was born in Welland, Ontario, on August 9, 1950. He had an unusual career plan, dropping out of high school to work with his father at the Canadian Press. I'm guessing their paper routes were side by side, but I'm probably wrong.

Years went by, and in 1975 Chris met another journalist guy named Scott Abbott. The two of them had been assigned to work together on the upcoming Summer Olympics in Montreal in 1976. They became buddies. Drinking buddies.

That's how they invented the Trivial Pursuit game, apparently. They were having a couple of beer and were trying to play Scrabble, even though a bunch of the letters were missing. They found out that alcohol doesn't increase your vocabulary, it only amplifies it. And somehow out of the chaos came a friendly competition about which of them had the largest bank of useless information.

Yet again we have an invention that is much more than meets the eye. Let's start with the name: Trivial Pursuit.

Now, we all know that the word *trivial* means "not important," "meaningless," "waste of time." In any other time in history, that would have been a negative. But not in the '80s. At that moment, trivial was cool, hip, saucy and a big breath of fresh air. Everything else was important back then—your career, your marriage, your life. The idea that these guys would call their game trivial was a head-turner. Felt good to snub your nose at society and spend some time doing something trivial.

Then you add the word *pursuit*, and now you've gone way over the top. The message is that not only is it okay to do something trivial, but you should actually go out there and *pursue* trivial things to do. Don't wait for the meaningless to come to you—get out there and go for it. *Carpe inutilis*—seize the useless.

And along with this rebellion came validation. All that dumb stuff that had been cluttering your mind for years and absolutely never came up in any conversation now had value. If you were the only guy in the room who knew stuff like the GDP of New Guinea, you were suddenly a genius.

What a fantastic windfall for all of the world's boring nerds. They were buying Trivial Pursuit in crazy numbers. They'd have Trivial Pursuit parties where there were ten or fifteen minutes of awkward conversation along with bizarre snacks and obscure soft drinks, and then the host would set about destroying his guests in the game. Now *that's* what I call fun.

Balderdash was designed by Canadians Laura Robinson and Paul Toyne. The game came out in 1984. It was sort of the board game version of a parlour game called Fictionary.

You play the game by making up false definitions for words nobody knows, and then trying to get the other players to "pick" your definition as the real one while trying to guess the actual definition yourself. It was a great way to practise lying, and has been recommended to anyone seeking a career in politics or timeshare sales.

The game has sold over fifteen million copies worldwide. The world has more balderdashers than ever.

Balderdash came out of a backlash to trivia games. All the people who had bluffed their way through life, pretending to know more than they did, were being regularly humiliated playing Trivial Pursuit. They needed a game that was geared to their strengths. Then along came Balderdash, where bravado and deception were rewarded and knowledge was, at best, of no value. This was the game for the "fake it till you make it" crowd. A game for people in sales or public relations or televangelism or any field where you need to make people feel good.

We played a similar version when I was in school, but it was called "What happened to your homework?"

The truth rarely works. People say they want the truth, but they're usually way more comfortable with a pleasant, credible lie. That's because the truth, and facts in general, tend to be disappointing. And when you're trying to make people feel good, disappointment is rarely gonna get you there.

Telling believable lies is a talent that takes years to perfect. It starts with sharing pieces of information that are factually correct but are missing the key elements that would turn them into bad news. "The oak tree next to your house was struck by lightning and fell to the ground, narrowly missing your garage." Information omitted: "It nailed your car."

Once you get that part down, you can gradually start introducing false information, "The oak tree next to your house was struck by lightning and fell to the ground, narrowly missing your garage. I understand the government has created a homeowners' fund that will award you up to fifty thousand dollars, no questions asked. By the way, I have a great investment opportunity, but the clock is ticking. I suggest you borrow against that subsidy and get it on the ground floor."

Over time, increase the percentage of the made-up stuff, and one day you will get to the point where virtually everything you say will be totally fabricated and yet have the eerie ring of truth. "Bats can make their own hearts stop beating for up to thirty-seven days." Wouldn't everybody enjoy that kind of fun? The inventors of Balderdash certainly thought so. And they were right. But the best part about Balderdash is that it taught us the most important part of being dishonest: credibility. "Lying is easy," U.S. President Richard Nixon said in 1973. "Getting people to believe the lie is the hard part."

To see the reigning Possum Lodge King of Balderdash in action, go to the Book of Inventions page at redgreen.com and click on "Balderdash."

TV CENSORSHIP
Tim Collings

T im Collings began work on the V-chip technology as a student at St. Francis Xavier University in Nova Scotia in 1990. (Have you noticed how many of these inventors have a connection to Nova Scotia? Don't know what it means, just wondered if you noticed it.)

After the 1989 mass shooting at École Polytechnique, he decided to try to restrict the kinds of harmful images children were exposed to through television. Tim—a dad himself—saw it as something parents should control, not the government or broadcasters. So with Tim's gizmo, the parents could decide what types of programming were shown or blocked on their home TV sets.

The unofficial code name for this software was Party Pooper. The way it works is different shows are given an adult rating based on language, violence and/or sexual content, and with a TV equipped with a V-chip, parents can filter out what is shown and what's not. The V-chip filters can be adjusted using a four-digit password, so Mom and Dad can watch whatever they want after the kids have gone to bed, but the kids still can't watch whatever they want after the parents go to bed.

✳ ✳ ✳

Okay, let me get this straight. Collings invented the V-chip so that parents can set the television to shut out whatever is not okay for their kids to watch. The television would now do this. So with this little doodad, the parents could feel even less guilty about not having to actually be around their kids.

When I was a kid, we also had something that decided what was okay for us to see or not see. We called her Mom. And since there was only one radio, and later one TV, in the house, whatever we were listening to or watching, so was she. It is sad to think that televisions and computers are raising our kids now.

I guess it is good that things like V-chips exist so that our new electronic parents at least have some kind of moral compass. If my uncle had a V-chip installed in his brain, that would have cut my twelve-year-old vocabulary in half.

Naturally, this particular invention takes us into the whole world of censorship and whether any person, even a parent, has the right to restrict what another person, even their kid, is allowed to see. I know the V-chip was designed to stop kids from watching certain shows, but it would also work on adults. If you don't know the code, you don't get to watch. So husbands could lock out the Food Network from their wives, and wives could do the same thing to prevent their husbands from watching Speedvision.

I'm not sure this approach even works anymore. Kids today see more X-rated stuff on their iPhones and hear worse language on the school bus than ever gets on television. Maybe the real value of the censorship is that it makes the parents feel better because at least they're not condoning their kids' exposure, while it also sends a message to the kids that their parents don't approve. When I was a kid, that just made me want to see it all the more.

Local free spirit Skunk Morrison moved the TV censorship initiative in a different direction. He had taken a correspondence course in electronics and had learned a lot from experimenting with the endless stream of used televisions and stereos that he sold from his van.

While visiting his brother-in-law, Skunk became aware of the V-chip that had been set up so that his nephews weren't allowed to accidentally see any prison programs that featured other members of the family. After sitting through five episodes of *The Brady Bunch*

Doug "Skunk" Morrison, Party Animal and Partly Animal

in a row, Skunk went home and created the X-chip. It had many similarities to the V-chip. It shut out programs and channels, and you needed to enter a code to override those barriers. But the conditions governing those restrictions were quite a bit different.

Skunk set up the X-chip so that only shows that had adult content, nudity, profanity, sexual situations and extreme violence were allowed to be seen. He also added a feature whereby no show could be viewed if it had a main character named Marcia. Even with this elaborate filtering system, Skunk noticed that once in a while a good, clean, family-oriented program would somehow sneak through. He called the local TV station to get them to be more specific in their disclaimers.

Skunk complained that when the message said, "The following program may contain scenes with foul language, nudity and sexual situations," the word *may* created an uncomfortable uncertainty. Skunk was not interested in sitting through the whole show and then finding out it didn't contain any of those things. He wanted them to replace the word *may* with *does* or *doesn't*.

Ultimately, the TV station stopped taking Skunk's calls and the X-chip was abandoned. Skunk had never applied for a patent, so he was out of luck when the X-chip resurfaced under the name HBO.

RED SAYS: The beauty of having a time machine is that it allows you to invent things that already exist.

UFO LANDING PAD

As part of Canada's centennial celebrations, the world's first UFO landing pad was constructed in St. Paul, Alberta, in 1967. I guess the town council was assuming the aliens speak English and are into geography, because the site features a map of Canada as well as a sign reading, "The area under the world's first UFO landing pad was designated international by the Town of St. Paul as a symbol of our faith that mankind will maintain the outer universe free from national wars and strife. That future travel in space will be safe for all intergalactic beings. All visitors from earth or otherwise are welcome to this territory and to the Town of St. Paul."

If there is ever a War of the Worlds, we can never blame it on the good people of St. Paul.

✳ ✳ ✳

Okay, there's a lot to think about here. It's one thing to reserve one of the larger Walmart parking spaces for UFOs only. It's a much bigger thing to dedicate a piece of property in a prime location and then cough up enough money to build a landing platform that would be functional and also attractive to the eye for the literally tens of tourists that might ultimately come to look at it. It seems like there would be so many unanswered questions with a project like this.

Aside from the obvious—*Why?*—there's the amount of guesswork that has to go into the design. The *U* in UFO stands for "unidentified" which is a fancy way to say "unknown," and there are plenty of those. What are they made of? How big are they? How heavy are they? Just because nobody sane or sober has ever seen one, it doesn't mean they're small. How big and strong does the landing pad have to be? How did anyone talk the town council into going along with this?

Let's look at it from the aliens' point of view. If they do exist and have the ability to visit other solar systems, out of the infinite universe of places to go to, what are the odds that they'd pick St. Paul, Alberta? Not that there's anything wrong with St. Paul, Alberta, but I was thinking they might want to visit Paris or Rome or London or New York before they dropped into the Calgary Stampede.

At first glance, you might think this means there are a whole bunch of people in Alberta who believe in UFOs. I think it's just the opposite. I don't think they believe in UFOs at all. If they did, they'd have used the money to monitor intergalactic activity so they could see a UFO coming and direct it to Saskatchewan.

Even if they went as far as building a landing pad, if they were serious, they'd have to man it 24/7. Which they didn't, 'cause they're not. No, my friends, this baby is just a tourist attraction. A fun way to put St. Paul on the map. I just hope that if UFOs ever *do* show up, they don't take offence at this little joke and blast us all off to Zorgon.

Naturally, this brings me to the bigger question of whether or not there is life on other planets. Scientists and astronomers have speculated for years that when you have an infinite universe with a limitless number of planets, that it is mathematically impossible for there not to be life on at least one other planet and probably on many.

That's because of what they call "probability." Probability is the ratio between how many of something you're looking for and how many there are. If you have three cards face down on the table and one of them is the ace of spades, you have a one-in-three chance of picking the ace of spades. But we all knew that the ace of spades was one of the three.

Not so with extraterrestrial life. The scientists base their probability on the endless supply of planets, not on knowing for sure there is life out there. So I say they're wrong. I say there is no other life form in any galaxy anywhere. I know this is a huge blow to all bad science-fiction movies. And there've been a few. But the fact that we haven't found life, or even signs of life, encourages me to say there isn't any.

As of nine o'clock this morning, there were 171,476 words in the English language. Mathematicians would tell you that means there's a one-in-171,476 chance that I'm going to say any of those words. Not true. I am not going to say the word *phlegm*. Ever. I just wrote it, but I didn't say it. And the fact that I've never said it doesn't make me more likely to say it. For the same reason there's no life on Pluto. Not even fleas.

I'm also questioning the million or so assumptions we've made to get this far. Let's start with the concept of flying saucers. Where did that come from? Maybe H.G. Wells thought of it after a domestic dispute. Maybe it comes from people looking at stars and thinking they kind of look like saucers. Which they don't. And yet the flying saucer is the supposed airship of choice from galaxies far, far away. They didn't build a *runway* in St. Paul, they built a *pad*. They're not expecting the spacemen to arrive in a 747. They're talkin' flying saucer.

Well, I don't see that happening, and here's why. There is no gravity in space. Because of that, there is no air. Because of that, there is no air pressure or resistance. Because of that, there is no lift and no friction. You could strap a jet engine to a Winnebago and it would glide through space like a javelin.

My point is that, in space, a flying saucer is as good a shape as any. But here on earth, we have gravity and air pressure and air resistance and since, at least as of this writing, St. Paul, Alberta, is still part of earth, it will have all three of those elements.

This is gonna make problems for a flying saucer. It did fine hurtling through space, but the hurtling phase will now be over and the hurting stage will now begin. That's because it will now be flying through air. And probably not very well. Because to fly through air for longer than ten seconds or so, you need to have lift.

Lift is what overcomes the pull of gravity. The normal way to create lift is with a wing (or see "Wonderbra," page 240). Our space shuttles have wings specifically for this purpose. A wing creates lift by having the top surface of the wing curved and longer than the bottom surface.

Because of that, the air that goes over the top gets deflected vertically, which creates a pocket of low pressure over the wing. A bit of a vacuum. But the bottom surface of the wing is flat, so the air pressure remains constant. The difference between those air pressures causes the wing, and the plane, to be pulled up by the pocket of low pressure. That's lift. Now look at the design of a flying saucer.

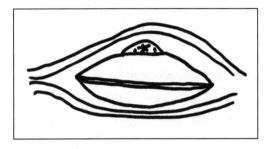

The upper and lower surfaces are the same size and shape. Ain't no lift happening there. So once the flying saucer enters the earth's atmosphere, the combination of air resistance and gravity would give it a flight pattern like this.

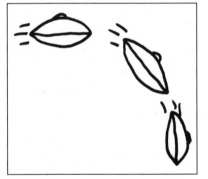

The vertical dive section at the end will probably be around five miles long, which, based on gravitational acceleration of thirty-two feet per second per second, would have it hitting the earth at around 1,200 miles an hour. I'm not sure the St. Paul landing pad could handle that. On the bright side, they'd have the deepest oil well in Alberta.

In one of our very first shows, the guys at the Lodge saw a UFO. To watch it, go to the Book of Inventions page at redgreen.com and click on "UFO."

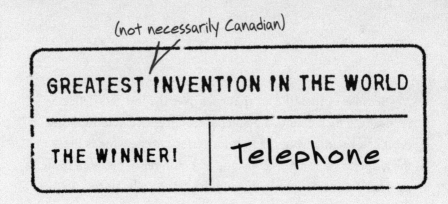

Pictured opposite is the guy who came up with the greatest invention in the world of all time ever. Oh sure, it had a modest beginning. It was a one-trick pony that needed networks of wires and switches and people to make it work. But over the years it showed itself to be such a necessary part of everyday life that 150 years after it was invented, it is not only still around but has also absorbed all of the jobs of every one of the other candidates I already listed in this book.

Today it's a calendar, a clock, a camera, a laptop, a video game, a flashlight, a remote control, a radio and a TV. And more things than that. And here's the best part: I've got one in my pocket. It's called a phone.

Thank Alexander Graham Bell—and chalk another big one up for Canada.

RATING: We have a winner!

UPHOLSTERY COUTURE

Eleanor Gauthier, Woman at Large

Although she had no formal training in dress design, Eleanor Gauthier decided to go into the world of fashion in the hopes of being able to make attractive formalwear for the fuller-figured woman.

Eleanor had discovered from personal experience that the flimsier materials, such as chiffon and silk, did not have the structural integrity to keep all body parts covered when doing many of the more popular modern dances. Eleanor had worn such dresses many times, and there had been a fair amount of fallout. While only getting one or two wearings out of any outfit, Eleanor noticed that her parents had never needed to have their couch recovered in the fifty years they'd owned it.

She then set her sights on designing sensible clothes for women in plus-sizes and having them made out of upholstery material—the tagline for her clothes was "We put the chest in chesterfield!" When she was unable to sell her designs to either haute couture boutiques or furniture stores, she decided to model them herself. She is pictured oppopsite wearing a ballroom gown made from upholstery that was a cotton/canvas blend. The outfit had double-stitched seams and came with arm covers, two throw cushions and a ten-year guarantee against mould and mildew. In the hope of getting more business, the salesman threw in the Scotchgarding, which was a bonus because Eleanor loved Scotch.

She wore the gown to the Governor's Ball, but was shocked to discover the governor's chairs were covered with exactly the same material (also pictured opposite). She suspected that the upholsterer had made her dress out of leftover fabric and asked the governor where he had purchased the chairs.

Unfortunately, he had forgotten to turn on his hearing aids and sat on her. She abandoned the upholstery-clothing business and went on a diet instead. Years later, the governor confided that Eleanor had always been his favourite recliner.

VARIABLE-PITCH PROPELLER
Wallace Rupert Turnbull

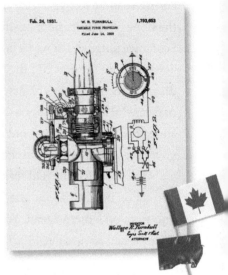

Wallace Rupert Turnbull was born in Saint John, New Brunswick, on October 16, 1870. Yet another inventor from the Maritimes. Must be the abundance of sea air and free time.

As a boy, Wally was always interested in aeronautics. By the time he was thirty-two he had built the first wind tunnel in Canada. Betcha didn't see that one coming. Which, incidentally, is the kind of thing you hear someone say in a wind tunnel. He received a medal from the Royal Aeronautical Society in 1909. He would have received it sooner but it blew away.

But it wasn't until 1927 that his most significant invention was tested: the variable-pitch propeller. Stop yawning. This was a big deal. Turnbull's variable-pitch propeller allowed the angle at which the blades spun to be changed, making taking off and landing much easier and more fuel-efficient. I bet you wouldn't have thought of that.

✳ ✳ ✳

A lot of books on inventions would leave out stuff like the variable-pitch propeller, but that's not the way we roll. Okay, maybe it's not an iron lung or a credible toupee, but it still deserves to be here. And what kind of a message does it send to our young people if we only recognize inventions that people care about?

The variable-pitch propeller is giving each of us a better life. Unless we never travel or ship anything by air. But even if we don't, we get the benefit of quieter skies because of Wally's little gizmo. Props make more noise when they're cutting more air. Remember your grandfather? Same thing.

So come down off your high horse and give Mr. Turnbull his due. If it wasn't for him, we'd all be dealing with single-pitch propellers. Imagine what kind of hell that would be.

Isaac Fluster of Possum Lake was an avid aviator and blue-sky thinker. While he had never gone to any type of flying school, he knew a guy who knew a guy who could get him an airplane of some kind, so he bought it and immediately became the most qualified bush pilot in the Possum Lake area.

Isaac's plane, the *Fig Newton*, was a four-propeller B-29 bomber. He added large storage tanks so he could use it to dust crops and put out forest fires. But his labelling on the release valves was hard to read, so he often would dump twenty tons of liquid fertilizer onto to a forest fire or drop ten thousand gallons of water onto a tomato crop. On one particularly memorable forest fire run, he pulled the wrong valve and dumped 2,500 gallons of aviation fuel into what up until that moment had been a manageable fire.

Isaac Fluster, Bush Pilot

The good news is that the immediate geometric increase in the size of the blaze assured Isaac of at least three more weeks of work. But of more immediate importance to him was the fact that he was now flying without fuel. Or as it's called in the aviation business, "gliding." This quickly turned into "diving" and then "crashing."

Although Isaac survived the crash, it detached two of his engines and one of his retinas. With his other eye, Isaac decided to see this in a positive light. He had become aware of Turnbull's variable-pitch propeller technology and, unencumbered by any education or humility, figured he could improve on it. Why would you stop at ten, thirty or even ninety degrees of adjustment when we all know there are 180 available?

So Isaac remounted the engines, but added gearing to the props so that their pitch could be adjusted 180 degrees. In other words, he could make them go from full forward to neutral to full reverse. He thought it would be a great stunt at the Possum Lake Air Show if, as he was flying over the crowd, he could put the two starboard engines into full reverse. And in fairness, it was a spectacle the survivors will never forget.

Isaac did a low-level pass over the stands doing about sixty knots when he adjusted the prop pitch and threw the starboard engines into full reverse. Even the oldtimers said they had never before seen a B-29 spin like a Frisbee, but unfortunately the manoeuvre caused the plane to replace its lift with drop.

Spectators who had remained a sensible distance away said, "It was an impressive routine, but he didn't exactly stick the landing." We've all heard that science is a great teacher, and on that day, Isaac and a large portion of the Possum Lake residents got a crash course in physics.

WALKIE-TALKIE
Donald Lewis Hings

Donald Lewis Hings was born in England in 1907, and came to Canada when he was three. At that age he could barely walkie *or* talkie. He messed around with electronics and communication on and off for the next twenty-nine years until, at the age of thirty-two, Donald filed for a patent for his portable radio system, which later became known as the walkie-talkie.

While he was waiting for the patent to be approved, Canada declared war on Germany. Donald was afraid his adopted country was overestimating the impact of his invention, but he later found out the two events were unrelated. Donald was sent to Ottawa, where he spent the next six years developing the walkie-talkie for military use. And eventually for every nerdy kid in the world.

❋ ❋ ❋

If you go through the list of inventions in this book, it's amazing to me how many of them are somehow related to finding ways for people to share information or feelings or art. From the foghorn to AM radio to

IMAX, and of course the telephone, it's not hard to tell that man is a social animal. Not every man and certainly not every Lodge member, but overall, people like to know they're not alone and that others are trying to ease their burden by either warning them of impending danger or sharing a song or a laugh or warning them of an impending song or a laugh. You gotta admit that most of us like to have somebody to talk to. Even miserable grumps would be lost without someone to hang up on.

While we have to salute the ingenuity and intelligence of Mr. Hings, the real bonus that came from the walkie-talkie was its new approach to communication. In order to limit the size and weight of each walkie-talkie unit, and also to remove the possibility of feedback, which happens whenever a live microphone gets too close to a speaker—or an in-law gets too close to a marriage— Donald ingeniously wired the speaker in such a way that when the talk button was pushed, the speaker became a microphone. It turned back into a speaker when the talk button was released.

That made it more than just an invention, it also was sending out a series of social statements. For starters, the default position of the walkie-talkie is listening mode, which flies in the face of thousands of years of human behaviour. For most people, the default position is talking or yelling or semi-comatose. Changing that to constantly being in listening mode was revolutionary and the kind of change that only a military environment could push through.

Next, because of the function of the talk button, you had to use a set of signals and codes to make the walkie-talkie work properly. With a telephone, which has a mouthpiece and an earpiece working at the same time, conversation is about the same as being right there with the person. Not so with the walkie-talkie. Because you can't hear them while you're talking, it's very possible to be talking away, only to find nobody's listening. You married women know what I mean.

So it was necessary to start with a short message to confirm that the intended person was listening. And inviting them to engage. The rule was for the caller to repeat the name of the recipient three times. "George. George. George. This is Martha. Come in." At which point, Martha would release the talk button so she could hear George's response: "Martha, this is George."

And then, according to the rules, George was obliged to say a code word that indicated that he was finished talking and was in full listening mode. That word is *over*.

And until Martha says the word *over*, George has to just listen—not interrupt, not make comments, not argue, not make excuses, just stand there and take it like a man. "George, I was emptying your pockets before doing the laundry and found a receipt for some kind of dune buggy or four-by-four or tractor or something and I'm wondering what that's all about. Over."

"It was supposed to be a surprise. Over."

"It was. Over."

"You're not mad, are you? Over."

"George, this is not the first time. Remember the submarine and the hot-air balloon? Over."

"I'll sell them. Over."

"It's too late. I don't want to do this anymore, George. Over."

"What does that mean? Are you saying it's over? Over."

"Yes . . . Over and out."

Apparently, even a walkie-talkie couldn't put George in a listening mode.

In an obvious attempt to get his name in the *Guinness Book of World Records*, local wingnut Eddy O'Bromowich used a

Edward "Fast Eddy"
O'Bromowich, Owner of the
World's Shortest Ties

walkie-talkie tuned to channel 16 to send the most ridiculous message ever received by RCMP Emergency Services. Here is the transcript of the call:

EDDY: Mayday! Mayday! Mayday!

RCMP: Come in. Over.

EDDY: It's a beautiful May day. Over.

RCMP: Can I help you, sir? Over.

EDDY: My dog is missing. Over.

RCMP: Not really our department. Over.

EDDY: I don't know s else to turn. Over.

RCMP: What is the dog's name? Over.

EDDY: Rover. Over.

RCMP: What does Rover look like? Over.

EDDY: Medium-sized, brown, and he is wearing a sweater. Over.

RCMP: A turtleneck? Over.

EDDY: Pullover. Over.

RCMP: Does he respond to any commands?

EDDY: Just roll over. Over.

RCMP: Where was the dog last seen? Over.

EDDY: Port Dover. Over.

RCMP: Do you live in Port Dover? Over.

EDDY: No. Hanover. Over.

RCMP: How did you lose track of the dog? Over.

EDDY: I laid down on a bench. Over.

RCMP: So you were having a sleep. Over.

EDDY: No, I had dropped my comb. Over.

RCMP: Where did you last see the dog in Port Dover? Over.

EDDY: The Water Street bridge. Over.

RCMP: On the bridge? Over.

EDDY: No, under. Over.

RCMP: We'll send an officer over. Over.

EDDY: What's his name? Over.

RCMP: Constable Grover. Over.

EDDY: Thanks. Over.

RCMP: I'll need to file a report. Please confirm that these facts are correct. I am dispatching Constable Grover to find Rover from Hanover wearing a pullover and missing in Port Dover. Over.

EDDY: Roger that. Over.

RCMP: And don't call me Shirley.

THE WONDERBRA
Moses Nadler

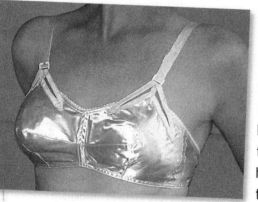

Wonderbra 1952 Version

The Wonderbra was first introduced to Canada by Moses "Moe" Nadler of the Montreal-based Canadian Lady Corset Company in 1939. He bought the name and the trademark from the U.S. and had the company's design team take it from there.

Over the next thirty years it became a huge hit as tastes shifted from girdles and corsets to a simpler, more comfortable bra. At least until the '60s, when everyone and everything was set free and women took a match to their bras, putting that "flame-retardant" label to the test.

Moses and his son Larry brought the Wonderbra to Europe and eventually the USA, and everywhere they went they would adapt the design to suit the attitudes and attributes of the women who wore them and the men who served as observers. Decades ahead of its time, the Wonderbra was really the first all-natural form of breast enhancement.

✳ ✳ ✳

Remember the days when it was taboo to even mention underwear. It was like we could only discuss the exterior of anything, especially ourselves. Everything beyond the outer layer of clothing was private. The nether regions were even referred to as "privates"—probably not in a military sense, because those kinds of privates do what they're told.

For a long, long time it was fashionable to be modest. Nobody would dare discuss their underwear, much less have it on display. And for a lot of people, any naked body other than their own was strictly and permanently out of bounds. And yet these same people had big families, so they were either leading a double life or things they did in the dark didn't count. I don't know where we're headed in the future, but I hope we don't get there before I do.

I'm not comfortable being around people who talk about their underwear or want to show it to me or want me to somehow adjust it. I appreciate a woman with a beautiful figure, but I don't care how she does it.

Let's be honest, the Wonderbra has to be the easiest invention ever. It's simple engineering, you've got a guaranteed market for the product and there are millions of teenaged boys who will volunteer to do the research for free. I bet the guys in the fitting room never missed a shift.

But in all fairness, the credit for the Wonderbra should have gone to local resident Herb Nordell, who used the same engineering and design to create similar products way before anyone else. Herb's problem was that he was not preoccupied with the female form, a lifestyle that was also years ahead of its time. He got the idea for his invention when his mother made a mistake while

Herb Nordell, Lodge Member and Brassiere Enthusiast

knitting caps for two-year-old local twins Rob and Robert Schlemmer. Instead of making the caps separately, she just knitted continuously from one to the other with the intention of cutting the middle chinstrap later.

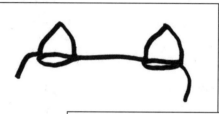

The parents stopped her from doing that because they liked the idea of the two caps attached together.

It made the twins easier to find in a crowd, and it supported the theory that two heads are better than one. It also made them deadly at games of red rover. The twins had always been close, but with the caps on, they were inseparable. Literally.

When Herb saw the caps, he instinctively
knew the design could be used in a better way.
His mind went immediately to football.

Herb had never been much of an athlete,
but he was allowed to be the Ball Boy of the
Possum Lake football team. (He preferred to be called the
Equipment Manager, so everyone called him the Ball Boy.) Herb
soon became aware that it was very difficult to carry more than
two footballs at a time. He figured he could solve that using the
cap design. All he had to do was make the cups out of a stronger
material, like cotton, add a couple of straps to use as handles, and
the football bra was born.

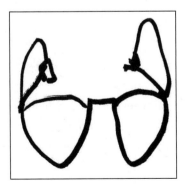

Herb knew that he needed some type of quick-release clasp on the bra so that the footballs could be released easily. Something that could be done with one hand. He added a double hook and eye attached to the ends of elastic straps. All Herb had to do was slip a cup onto each end of the football, engage the hooks and pick the unit up by the carrier straps.

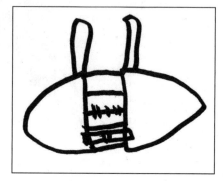

With this new system, Herb could carry four balls in each hand.

The next step was to have different sizes, as not all footballs are the same. Herb created the A, the double-A, the triple-A, the NFL and the Super Bowl. The CFL has even bigger balls, so Herb came out with his largest bra ever, the Grey Cups.

The concept never caught on, but Herb was named Local Inventor of the Year by his mom. A few years after the taunting died down, Herb decided that the flaw in his approach was that he was thinking too small. Or maybe not at all. In any case, he decided to go big or go home. And he should have gone home.

Instead, he used the football bra technology and supersized it into a self-propelled amusement park ride for kids of all ages. With an old swing set, a couple of pup tents and thirty feet of rubber, the Swing Bra was born. The first step is to remove the swings from a swing set, leaving the large A-frame of pipes.

Use a front-end loader—
or a group of friends who have
no lives—to reposition the
A-frame so that it's about
twenty-five feet from something firmly attached to the
ground, like a tree or a telephone pole or a really fat guy.

Next, assemble the two pup tents,
turn them over and cut out the floors.

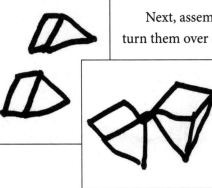

Now attach two
adjacent corners of
the pup tent together,
reminiscent of the
twins' knitted caps.

Now you'll need
some type of strong
straps (fire hoses work great and are easy to swipe while the
firemen are upstairs playing pinochle). From the upper corner
of each tent, run the straps up and over the A-frame and
connect them to the two outside corners of the pup tents. That
way, they will lift *and* separate. From one of those same corners,
run your strip of rubber around the pole and attach it to the

other corner. Shorten the length so that it holds the tents up but allows them to hang right.

And it's just that easy. Get a friend or acquaintance or somebody who owes you money. Each of you gets into a pup tent. Together you walk into the tents backwards, creating tension in the pole strap, and then just lift your feet and get this party started.

Herb built the Swing Bra right next to the cenotaph in downtown Possum Lake, and he and his buddies had a lot of fun with it until the cops showed up. Herb was forced to dismantle the swing and abandon the concept and design. Sad that he had the whole brassiere thing right there in his hands but couldn't see it.

They say it was his own fault. At the height of the Swing Bra project, when Herb and his pal were swinging away to beat the band, a passerby turned to his partner and said, "Look at those boobs!" Herb was oblivious.

RED SAYS: All inventors should be able to recognize things by their smell—chlorine, gasoline, propane and fear.

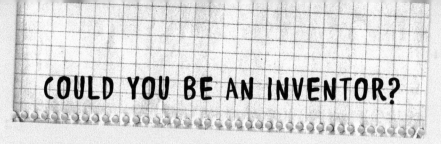

COULD YOU BE AN INVENTOR?

Take the following quiz to find out if you have what it takes to be the next great Canadian inventor.

CIRCLE ONE
(Please do NOT circle both)

Do you read books about stuff?	Yes	No
Do people generally think of you as smart?	Yes	No
Are you consistently in the top third of your class?	Yes	No
Do you have any post-secondary school education?	Yes	No
Do you have any post-elementary school education?	Yes	No
When playing a sport that needs ten people on each team, are you often picked between first and ninth?	Yes	No
Do you like to entertain people?	Yes	No
Do you like to educate people?	Yes	No
Do you like to socialize with people?	Yes	No
Do you like people?	Yes	No
Do people like you?	Yes	No
Are you successful in most things you attempt?	Yes	No

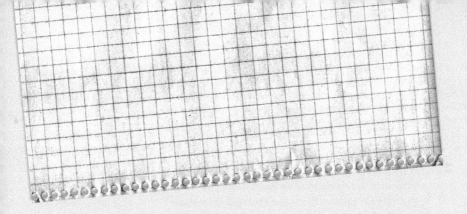

Do you ever get lonely?   Yes   No

Would you call yourself a team player?   Yes   No

Do you see value in research to find out what the
majority of people want and/or need?   Yes   No

Does it bother you when you are called a moron?   Yes   No

Are you interested in acquiring tremendous wealth?   Yes   No

Are you interested in acquiring modest wealth?   Yes   No

Are you interested in scraping by?   Yes   No

Are you interested in anything other than your
invention?   Yes   No

Are you Canadian?   Yes   No

RESULTS: If you answered yes to anything but the last question, you have almost no chance of being an inventor. However, if that declaration doesn't bother you, you may still have a chance.

IMAGE CREDITS

115: NASA Goddard Space Flight Center
117: Australian National Maritime Museum, Samuel J. Hood Studio Collection
122: CBC Still Photo Collection
127: Chris Rand / cc via Wikimedia Commons
128: Arthur S. Goss / Library and Archives Canada
131: Tom Watson / NY Daily News Archive via Getty Images
134: The Met, Gift of Joel Snyder, 1994
139: McCord Museum / cc via Flickr
141: Library of Congress Prints and Photographs Division
144: ver abajo / cc via Wikimedia Commons
146: The Finnish Museum of Photography
147: McGarva Photo Collection of Pictou County Characters
151: Ltisdall / cc via Wikimedia Commons
153: angela n / cc via Flickr
155: Photocapy / cc via Flickr
159: Jim Rees / cc via Wikimedia Commons
160: Library of Congress Prints and Photographs Division
165: Guilhem Vellut / cc via Flickr
168: Peter Burger / cc via Wikimedia Commons
172: Milton Historical Society / Halton Images
173: Library of Congress Prints and Photographs Division
177: Archives Montreal / cc via Flickr
185: Cardiff Council Flat Holm Project / cc via Flickr
186: National Film Board of Canada / Library and Archives Canada
194: Library and Archives Canada
196: Library of Congress, C.M. Bell Studio Collection
198: Library and Archives Canada
200: Johnny Silvercloud / cc via Flickr
201: Bettmann / Getty Images
207: Smithsonian Institution Archives
208: Hockey Hall of Fame / Library and Archives Canada
211: University of Washington Libraries, Digital Collections
212: Library of Congress Prints and Photographs Division
215: Basil Zarov / Library and Archives Canada
217: Scott / cc via Flickr
223: Heterodyne at English Wikipedia / cc via Wikimedia Commons
229: Moffett Studio / Library and Archives Canada
238: McGarva Photo Collection of Pictou County Characters
240: Mattnad / cc via Wikimedia Commons
242: Bergen Public Library

INDEX

ACKNOWLEDGEMENTS

I can't take all the credit for the writing of this book. Well I could, but the lawyers are strongly advising against it. So in the interest of avoiding a series of expensive frivolous lawsuits that would probably not end well, I would like to acknowledge and thank, or possibly just acknowledge, Steve Smith and David T. Smith for their research and writing contributions on this project. I'm not exactly sure how much of the book they wrote but it's somewhere between 90% and 101%. I could have written the whole book myself but I think this was a better choice and I know the publisher agrees with that. In any case, I got my name on the cover and they didn't so who cares?

ABOUT THE AUTHOR

Red Green is a self-appointed master handyman and outdoors-man, a weekly participant in Canada's socialized medical system, and a firm believer that no repair job should outlive you. He enjoys taking things that were intended for one purpose and using them for something completely different.

He is oblivious to failure. (Something that could change once he experiences success.)

He is either the youngest old man or the oldest young man you will ever meet.